London's Hurricane

by Mark Davison and Ian Currie

The great storm of October 16, 1987 was a meteorological event that the people of London will never forget. It paralysed communications, plunged thousands of homes into darkness, brought down telephone wires and destroyed houses and factories. Trees fell everywhere; in surburban streets, in parks and commons, on top of cars. The Stock Exchange ceased trading, so did the Bank of England. City offices closed and few schools remained open. It was the most destructive day the capital had known since the Blitz and there was a blitz-like spirit about the way London faced up to this surprise adversity. *London's Hurricane* is a follow-up to the hugely successful book *In The Wake of The Hurricane* which became a runaway best seller for eight successive months. *London's Hurricane* provides a fascinating and historical photographic record of a night which has already taken its place in London's folklore.

Froglets Publications

The grove of limes was an attractive feature of the Barrack Field at Woolwich. These two pictures tell a sad story.

2

3

Part of the proceeds from the sale of this book will be donated to the London Wildlife Trust and other woodland appeals in the London boroughs.

Published by Froglets Publications Ltd, Brasted Chart, Westerham, Kent TN16 1LY.

Telephone: (0959) 62972. Fax: (0959) 65365

© Froglets, 1989

ISBN 0-9513019-3-4

*This book was fully produced by
Pen & Ink Publicity Services,
9 Cannon Lane, Tonbridge, Kent TN9 1PP.*

*Front cover photograph:
Big Ben on October 16, 1987. Photograph: John McBean*

*Back cover photograph:
The Bayswater Road area of Hyde Park on the morning of the
hurricane. Photograph by: Hyde Park staff.*

Edited and designed by: Bob Ogley

"London's Hurricane" is dedicated to professional photographers and particularly those who work for London's daily and regional newspapers. Rarely do they receive the credit they deserve for recording history as it happens. Without their expertise and skill this book would not have been possible.

Acknowledgements

Daily, evening and weekly newspaper editors in London have helped considerably by allowing us to look through their own special storm reports which have served as leads in the preparation of this book. We are also grateful to the staff of all the London boroughs who have generously spared us time by giving us vital storm statistics. Great assistance has come from London Libraries, The Guildhall, the National Trust, the staff of the London parks, and all the London hospitals.

We are also indebted to the following:

The Tree Council (Anne Edwards)
Norman Smith
Paul Acres
Sass Tuffin
British Waterways Board
Meteorological Office
London Weather Centre
M. Volk
Mike Robinson
Caroline Hempstead-International Stock Exchange
British Telecom
Buckingham Palace
Lewisham Local History Centre
Tom Morris
Chris Wood
John McBean
A. Beckman
Port of London Authority
Ian Brearly
Climatological Observers Link
K. Ward
Evelyn Prideaux
N. Elms
David Wallis
David Jones
K. Ward
Mr & Mrs Wheatley
Jenny Currie
Mrs M. Stone
Zoo Operations — Ltd — Regents Park Zoo
Hubert Chesshyre
Ron Howes
Neil O'Conner-Baliffof
N. W. Jackson
Mrs J. Adams
Mr J. Buttress
Captain Fisher
David Lloyd
L. R. T. News
Rees Thomas
Timothy Honnor

Mike Robinson
Bow Neighbourhood
Robert Cork
Doug Morley
Paul Simons, Harrow
Tony Payne, Harrow
Miss Smeaton
Friends of Richmond Park
Hampton Court staff
Terry Gorgh
G. Cooke
Roy Smith
Hounslow Library
Eddie Mulholland
Patsy Fagan
Gerald Isaaman
David Tippett-Wilson, Hook
Tony Howard, RBK
N & M Davison, Hook
Paul Gerkard
Ben Murray
Margaret Givan
Barbara Gower
Bob Heron
Neil McGinn
David Allen, Richmond
Kevin and Linda Mills
Benedick Devlin
Brian Curle, Kensington
Helen Grimwade
Barbara Dack
R. Jones, Fulham
Paul Adams, Long Ditton
Oriel Robinson
Ben and Doris Murray
J. Stebbings, W12
Sue Messenger
C. H. Jones
John Powell, Sutton
Gordon Allis
W. Harvey, Ewell
Liz Cook LFB

*And finally to **Fern Flynn** of Froglets whose cheerfulness, advice and industry has inspired us all.*

When London's heart missed a beat

by Bob Ogley, author of the book *In The Wake of The Hurricane* which covered the trail of the storm across Southern England. Bob's book became a national bestseller and remained in the top ten list for eight consecutive months.

IT has been said that Londoners will never forget the night of the hurricane. That is not accurate. Thousands of deep sleepers were unaware of the whooshing and the howling. They missed the sound of empty milk bottles cartwheeling down the road and the incessant clatter of dustbinlids. They didn't know that families were being evacuated from skyscrapers, that their own car in the road outside was squashed under a plane tree. They knew nothing of the drama on the Thames, in the hospitals, in fire brigade head-quarters and in the emergency control centres, established at the dead of night.

Yes, thousands slept through the most violent storm for 250 years — but they will never forget the morning that followed. London was paralysed. There was no electricity, roads were blocked, homes were damaged, cars were crushed. There were no flights from Heathrow, few buses or trains. The underground service was crippled. Many people were injured and, sadly, two had died in the night.

It all happened in a few hours of wild fury. The power of the wind in the London boroughs uprooted an estimated 250,000 trees and statistics abounded as the final cost was evaluated in millions of pounds. It was to be the most expensive night London has ever known in peacetime.

The great storm is now history but in pubs, clubs, homes and offices it has remained one of the great talking points. The Stock Exchange ceased trading and so did the Bank of England. City offices and factories closed. Commuters had a day off and so did most schoolchildren. Life came briefly to a standstill as London's heart missed a beat.

Mark Davison and Ian Currie have put together this fascinating history of London's Hurricane in photographic form. They have spoken to ecologists, meteorologists and appeal organisers. New pictures have been published alongside those taken directly after the storm. Together they build up into a total dramatic picture of a historic night, now part of London's folklore.

There are a few things which strike fear into the heart of other-wise logical and level-headed adults and one of them is a violent storm. Many of those who were needed in the night — policemen, firemen, ambulancemen and council staff — were terrified. Not only were trees falling but corrugated iron sheets were flying through the air and scaffolding poles were being thrown about like javelins. Our heroes went out to the rescue of others. It really was in the spirit of the blitz.

Some of these pictures are already famous. The tree making a trunk call outside the Albert Hall and the demolition of the transit van right under a board advertising the merits of transit vans are two. The Pimlico picnickers, the Tilbury crane and the desolation in Victoria Park are others. Readers will have their own favourites.

Sadly in London there were two fatalities. Terrence Marrin, who was dossing out in Lincoln's Inn Fields was killed by a tree. Robert Doke died when a tree fell on the car he was driving. He was in Croydon, eight miles from his home in Catford.

The story from each of the 32 boroughs is given in a simplified fashion with a storm chart. In bare statistics this tells of the drama in each locality, the cost of clearing up and the replanting pro-gramme. Each borough has its own systematic call-out system for workers, triggered by requests for help. The machinery worked well that night.

Although the great storm was at the time seen to be a disaster, and it was indeed a catastrophe for those gardeners who lost valu-able and important trees, carefully nurtured over the years, we can appreciate that benefits have, nonetheless, followed in its wake.

Many people have recognised for the first time the importance of trees and begun to take a greater interest in them; perhaps this may have given an additional impetus to the developing concern for the environment.

The response of Londoners to tree appeals was magnificent. The Evening Standard alone raised more than £60,000, supported by a wonderful diversity of endeavour from the cast of 42nd Street to the staff of The Treasury, from the General Synod to G.I. Brides in Colorado, from carol-singing solicitors in Lincoln's Inn to poetic schoolchildren at Palmer's Green. Every borough had its own well-supported appeal.

The Victorian legacy to Londoners was trees lining almost every street, softening the harshness of bricks and mortar and turning London into one of the leafiest capitals in Europe. Unfortunately, the trees planted were of necessity usually planes as these were best able to withstand the pollution of bygone London. In their maturity they darkened many a square and front rooms lost the light of sun.

Now that some of the old giants are gone and with London's cleaner air we have been given the best opportunity in 100 years to replant in far greater variety to the benefit and enjoyment of all.

A disfigured survivor in the Bellingham Play Park at Winsford Road, Catford.

Photograph by D.G. Wallis, Bellingham.

This willow weeps no longer. A tangled scene beside the pond on the grassy acres of Blackheath.

7

Chaos in the heart of London. This was the scene in Villiers Street, Charing Cross on the morning of the storm.

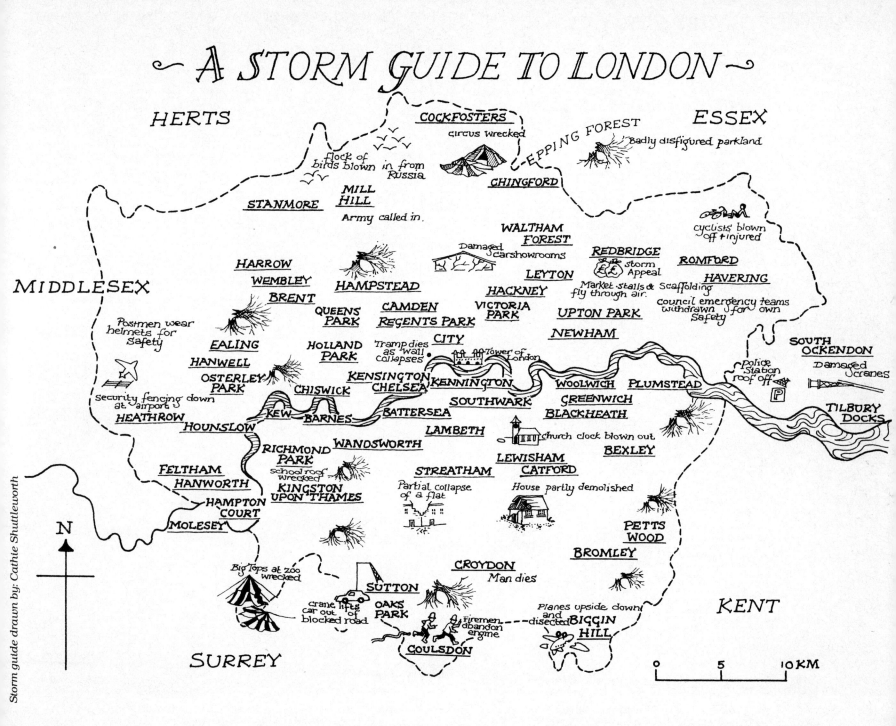

~ A STORM GUIDE TO LONDON ~

HERTS

ESSEX

COCKFOSTERS
circus wrecked

EPPING FOREST

Badly disfigured parkland

Flock of birds blown in from Russia

CHINGFORD

MILL HILL

STANMORE

Army called in.

WALTHAM FOREST

cyclists blown off + injured

MIDDLESEX

HARROW

WEMBLEY

BRENT

HAMPSTEAD

Damaged carshowrooms

REDBRIDGE

storm Appeal

ROMFORD

HAVERING

LEYTON

HACKNEY

Market stalls & fly through air.

Scaffolding

Postmen wear helmets for safety

QUEENS PARK

CAMDEN

REGENTS PARK

VICTORIA PARK

council emergency teams withdrawn for own safety

EALING

HOLLAND PARK

CITY

UPTON PARK

NEWHAM

HANWELL

OSTERLEY PARK

Tramp dies as wall collapses

Tower of London

SOUTH OCKENDON

Police Station roof off

Damaged cranes

KENSINGTON

CHELSEA

KENNINGTON

Woolwich

PLUMSTEAD

security fencing down at airport

CHISWICK

HEATHROW

HOUNSLOW

KEW

BARNES

BATTERSEA

SOUTHWARK

GREENWICH

BLACKHEATH

TILBURY DOCKS

LAMBETH

church clock blown out

WANDSWORTH

RICHMOND PARK

school roof wrecked

STREATHAM

LEWISHAM

CATFORD

BEXLEY

FELTHAM

HANWORTH

KINGSTON UPON THAMES

Partial collapse of a flat

House partly demolished

HAMPTON COURT

MOLESEY

PETTS WOOD

N

BROMLEY

Big Tops at zoo wrecked

CROYDON

Man dies

KENT

crane lifts car out of blocked road

SUTTON

OAKS PARK

Firemen abandon engine

Planes upside down and disected

BIGGIN HILL

COULSDON

SURREY

0   5   10 KM

Storm guide drawn by: Cathie Shuttleworth

9

Sorry tale of mangled cars

HUNDREDS of Londoners woke up after a night of restlessness to find they had no telephone, no electricity and, in the road outside, a motor car unbelievably mangled. These pictures tell a sorry tale and they represent a scene that faced motorists in every borough on the morning of the storm.

Chelsea and Kensington Arts and Library Services

Cheyne Row, near the Albert Bridge. Jane Asher's car was another victim in this road.

Photograph by: Croydon Advertiser

Photograph by: Paul Gerkard

The insurance company decided this one was a write-off! It was parked overnight in Monks Orchard Road, Shirley, Croydon.

The wooden spear appeared from the garden beside Half Moon Lane, Herne Hill. No-one was hurt.

More than 200 cars in the borough of Ealing were damaged. This was a write-off along with 50 others.

A resident of Gloucester Road, Ealing who enjoys sleeping on car bonnets had to share this metro with a sleeping tree. The slumbers were interrupted by photographer Mark Kehoe.

Another one for the breakers' yard. This mangled victim was in Munster Road, Teddington.

South London in turmoil

Police Constable Stuart Rashworth suffered a broken nose when a tree fell on his car while he was driving to work at Clapham Police Station.

Concrete balconies on two flats in Sherland Gardens, Willowbrook Estate, Peckham, collapsed, plunging 30 feet.

There were many cases of trees on cars, but police found a car perched on a tree in Central Hill, Upper Norwood.

Peckham Rye Park became the graveyard for hundreds of trees before they were taken away in relays of lorries.

The roof of Brandlehow Junior School was partly ripped away and the school's 190 pupils had to stay at home. One classroom was extensively damaged.

A chimney crashed through three floors of the Three Stags pub in Kennington, coming to rest in the basement. The roof caved in, leaving a bill for £¼ million.

A rare Judas tree, over 100 years old, in the grounds of Dulwich Picture Gallery fell. It was planted in 1865.

A man escaped death by inches when a chimney crashed into his bedroom. Tom Measures pulled his disabled wife, Eileen, 55, to safety fearing the roof would collapse.

At the height of the storm, opportunist burglars looted shops in Brixton while power cuts silenced burglar alarms. Furniture was taken from a store in Acre Lane, jewellery stolen from H. Samuels and £500 of goods snatched from Curry's in Electric Avenue.

A house collapsed in Villa Road, Brixton and the roof of a block of flats on Stockwell's Studleigh Estate had to be weighed down with tarpaulins and sacks of salt.

Nearly 200 trees fell on Clapham Common and 100 in Battersea Park.

Newsagent Bhupen Patel lay unconscious for 20 minutes after being hit on the head by a shop balcony while opening his shop in Leigham Court Road, Streatham at 4.15am. An old man saw his hand sticking out and helped him to safety.

A Southwark scaffolding firm offered to deliver 'good burning' timber off-cuts to South London bonfire parties for nothing.

Torrential rain in the days following the storm led to 200 flood calls in South West and South East London. At Forest Hill, the South Circular was impassable. Basements were swamped in Tooley Street and in Bermondsey, drains were blocked by storm debris, causing flooding.

Photograph by: Patsy Fagan

Don't worry, luv — we're on our way. There's been a bit of a diversion at Clapham Junction!

Photograph by: Stanmore and Pinner Observer

Photograph by: Wembley Observer

There were few buses on the morning of the storm. This is Brook Avenue, Wembley Park, seen from a different angle.

A passing tree seeks shelter. This is Honeypot Lane, Stanmore.

The junction of Old Kent Road and East Street, Walworth — a temporary obstruction.

14

Photograph by: Patsy Fagan

The root holes of these trees on Wandsworth Common are closely inspected. In the borough, 43 roads were blocked and the Council was faced with a bill for £1.5 million.

Workmen had to remove these buckled scaffolding poles at Battersea, piece by piece. What bravery!

Photograph by: Jeremy Young

More than 100 trees fell in Brockwell Park, including this enormous Lombardy poplar. The Friends of Brockwell Park offered to help with the clear-up but this was rejected by Lambeth Council on safety grounds. Today, serenity has returned to this 124-acre park.

Sorry I'm late at the office. I had to walk and there was this wall to climb over on St. John's Hill, Clapham Junction!

Photograph by: Patsy Fagan

A nightclub canopy at Clapham which gave up the ghost.

Photograph by: Patsy Fagan

Adrian Mark of Strathclyde Road, Streatham looks at life on the other side.

Photographs by Eddie Mulholland

All 84 families living in this London tower block were evacuated after brick walls were sucked out of the the 13th floor. The wind left a vast gaping hole, just two feet from where David and Christine Wood were sleeping. The drama occurred at Sirinham Point on the Ashmole Estate, Kennington. For months after the storm families lived with relatives, or in cramped bed and breakfast accommodation, until Lambeth Borough Council declared the tower block safe.

Sirinham Point tower block. On the 13th floor David and Christine Wood had an aerial view of London they could have done without. A stereo, drinks cabinet and bedding were sucked through the hole.

Photograph by: Eddie Mulholland

David Wood on the 13th floor at Sirinham Point. He and his wife were lucky — they held on tight.

Windy in Wandsworth

A police officer on patrol in Battersea Park noticed the top of the Buddhist Temple pagoda rocking dangerously in the night. He alerted Wandsworth Borough Council who sent a crane to rescue the monument as the wind grew in intensity.

In Bristol Gardens, Putney Heath, a family was saved from serious injury because they slept so soundly. During the night a chimney stack collapsed through the roof and into the kitchen. Firemen told them there had been a violent storm.

It took Wandsworth council workmen several hours to clear fallen trees from The Avenue on Clapham Common. They worked in two shifts with chain saws, heavy lifting gear and lorries. Just as they finished the job three Lambeth council men arrived with a wheelbarrow.

There were a number of territorial disputes in the days and weeks which followed the storm. Local councils were at a loss to know what to do with the excess timber they had gathered and the equivalent of a customs control point was set up near the Albert Bridge.

An estimated 5,000 trees were destroyed on council-owned land in Wandsworth. More than 1,000 trees were considered to be dangerous and 20,000 required extensive surgery. In addition 1,500 saplings needed to be re-staked.

There was a shortage of saplings in Wandsworth and replacement trees were ordered from Holland. An extensive tree-planting programme was drawn up involving 14,000 trees at a cost of £1,531,000.

No through road! This is New Road, Abbey Wood, Belvedere on the morning of the storm.

Photograph by D. R. Morley

Photograph by: John Stuart, Banstead Herald

Pupils arrive at Fenstanton Infants and Junior Modern School, Tulse Hill only to discover they can have the day off. This delightful news was given to thousands of children all over London. Many schools were seriously damaged.

London's commuter belt became a wilderness overnight. This was the scene at Bolters Lane, Banstead, Surrey.

This is Brunswick Park between Peckham and Camberwell. In the background is St. Giles' Hospital.

Photograph by: Sevenoaks Chronicle

The former Battle of Britain fighter station at Biggin Hill in the Borough of Bromley, which is still an RAF base, suffered damage amounting to thousands of pounds. Eight privately owned aircraft were smashed, four written off and one sliced in half.

Across the borough of Bromley trees with white crosses were waiting to be removed. This photograph was taken in Beckenham Place Park six months after the storm.

Photograph by N. Elms.

Churches fared badly in the storm losing tiles, masonry, stained glass windows and pinnacles. This one at Stepney was struck by a tree.

Control by candlelight

CANDLES had to be brought out at the Greater London area ambulance co-ordination centre, Waterloo, when the emergency generator failed. Ambulance crews worked fearlessly through the night answering 700 calls between midnight and 9.00 a.m. on the Friday morning. Ambulances found roads blocked by fallen trees and masonry. Typical injuries were cuts from flying glass, shock, and those caused by road accidents such as people driving into fallen trees and debris.

London in the dark

MOST of London's electricity supplies were cut at the peak of the storm when the Central Electricity Generating Board's national grid failed. The London Electricity Board's 1.8 million homes, shops, and offices were blacked out for several hours. In and around the capital, most of the cables are underground, so long-term problems like those experienced in Surrey and Sussex were avoided. The LEB area stretches from near Loughton, Essex in the north to New Malden and Bromley in the south. Supplies were back on to many premises by 9 a.m.

12,400 emergency calls

The Metropolitan Police were inundated with calls for assistance. They recorded 12,400 emergency calls and at Wandsworth, at one stage, there were 19 callers on hold. Tooting police station had to go on emergency generators when their mains supply was knocked out at 3.30 a.m. Streatham police thought their computer system would 'blow up' as a torrent of 14,000 messages flooded in, and an officer told the Putney Guardian: "Thank God it happened at night". Wimbledon Police somehow answered 520 calls in one night.

No cash in the walls

THOUSANDS of bank cash-card machines were inoperative because of the power cuts hitting the computerised system.

Photograph by: Sass Tuffin

Mrs Prideaux of Lewisham Park Road was awoken by the sound of the wind howling around her upstairs maisonette. The bedroom window caved in showering her with glass so she made her way downstairs to the living room where she heard the wind tearing off roofing material, and hurling it against the window. Outside, falling trees caused havoc.

Photograph by: South East London and Kentish Mercury

Photograph by: D. G. Wallis

The gable end of this house in Bellingham Green, Catford was sucked out and deposited by the front door. Mrs Wheatley who was five months' pregnant at the time was showered with plaster and debris and her husband, who was downstairs, watched with astonishment as tiles were ripped off the roof and thrown over the garden. It was only at daylight that the full extent of the damage was realised. The Wheatleys' house is now restored but the couple will never forget that night.

The wind blew in the shop front of Broadway Reproductions in Catford Road, Catford, smashing furniture, windows and shop fittings, and leaving behind a bill for thousands of pounds.

Tower blocks overlook the devastation in Lewisham Park.

Photograph by N. Elms.

The National Maritime Museum at Greenwich escaped with only minor damage but 250 trees fell in the park. Today, much of the former serenity has returned.

Another violent storm

STAFF at the Science Museum in South Kensington arranged to show a film called Violent Storms on the day after the hurricane. The museum stressed that the film had been organised five months earlier and the timing was "pure coincidence".

A new Volvo estate belonging to actress Jane Asher was damaged by a falling lime tree in Cheyne Walk, Chelsea.

Warm-hearted residents of the Royal Borough of Kensington and Chelsea were quick to respond to the Tree Fund Appeal. By the end of 1988, 126 trees had been replaced at a cost of £8,500. Donations came from the Gas Board, the Electricity Board and Charringtons, the brewers.

The borough council had to commandeer a crane to remove a massive tree which fell across the busy Cromwell Road at 4am.

Photograph by: Kensington and Chelsea Post Group

The famous statue of Achilles looms above a jungle of fallen planes in Hyde Park. When it was unveiled on June 18, 1822, women were shocked at its nakedness, size and high elevation, and later a fig leaf was added. On October 16, 1987, whole branches covered the lower region of the statue, which stands on a site chosen by King George IV.

A small problem for pedestrians at Collingham Gardens, South Kensington. The motorist had a bigger problem.

Littering streets or defacing street furniture is an offence with a penalty of £100, says the sign. Here, at Kenway Road by the A4 in South Kensington, the culprit moved on quickly.

The grounds of St. Lukes Church, Chelsea — strewn with debris and fallen trees.

Chelsea Embankment and, across the river, the redundant Battersea Power Station.

Photograph by: Press Association

*A London plane tree makes a trunk call at the telephone kiosk
outside the Victoria and Albert Museum.*

Photograph by: Jerry Munson

*Lesley Hussain was alseep at her home in Dartmouth Park Road,
Kentish Town when a chimney crashed through four floors. She got
caught up in the avalanche and plunged with her bed 40ft from the
second floor into the basement. Firemen spent nearly three hours
trying to rescue her. Her father-in-law Dr Mumtaz Hussain, who was
sleeping on the ground floor, also had to be rescued. Lesley was
admitted to hospital with severe bruises.*

Logs and foliage represent one great tree which caused chaos in Redcliffe Square, West Brompton.

World nearly ends

MRS Barbara Dack lives in a penthouse flat on the 17th floor of the World's End tower block overlooking the River Thames at Chelsea. Her son, Keith, aged 17, who was sleeping on the settee was showered with great pieces of pointed glass which had been torn from the lounge window by the force of the wind. This is Barbara Dack's account of a terrifying night.

"I was awakened by my son who told me to move away from the window. He had cuts on his neck and tucked into the settee where he had been sleeping were six-inch long shards of glass which had narrowly missed his jugular vein. We tried to go back into the lounge but the door wouldn't open, such was the weight of the wind. The noise was terrible. We live 17 floors high so you can imagine the fear we suffered all night. I don't think I slept. In the morning we cleared up the mess and my window was boarded up. I will never forget that night".

Photograph by: Mark Lawson

39

STORM GUIDE TO THE LONDON BOROUGHS

Borough	Square Miles	Population (1981)	Trees lost in Public Places	Cost of Clear-up	Facts
BARNET	35	292,331	4,500+	£200,000+	Hendon Town Hall received 2,000 calls for help in three days. Army help clear roads in Mill Hills.
BARKING & D'HAM	13	150,175	5,000	£2,000,000	12,000 calls from council tenants. £50,000 damage to street lighting. £1m damage to council homes.
BEXLEY	23	214,818	75,000	£4,000,000	Scheme to re-plant 25,000 trees in two years. Free tree offered to residents if they plant it where passers-by can see it.
BRENT	17	251,527	4,500	£500,000+	150 trees crashed onto homes. First alert 1am. 19-man team worked 26 hours non-stop, clearing up borough.
BROMLEY	59	294,451	15,000	£1,500,000	300 council men at work by 3am. 19,000 replacement trees planted by September 1989.
CAMDEN	8	171,563	1,000+	£1,500,000	200 council staff involved in clear-up.
CITY	1	5,893	100		
CROYDON	33	316,557	75,000	£8,200,000	3,500 council homes damaged. 100 roads blocked. 75% of schools shut.
EALING	21	280,042	3,393	£500,000	200 cars damaged. About 50 written off.
ENFIELD	31	258,825	1,200	£78,000	
GREENWICH	18	211,806	2,000	£2,600,000	Keep-out signs nailed up outside all parks and woods, due to danger, 1,000 emergency calls to council.
HACKNEY	8	180,237	2,600	£2,000,000	Lost many rare trees.
HAMM & FULHAM	6	148,054	1,200+	£500,000	Plans to replace all trees were drawn up.
HARINGEY	12	203,175	2,900+	£550,000	Five per cent of tree total lost. 100 schools shut. 'Terrific regeneration of woodland floor'.
HARROW	20	195,999	6,000+	£150,000+	Parks staff, working six days a week, planted 5,700 trees by the spring of 1988.
HAVERING	45	240,318	5,000+	£1,000,000+	Emergency control room opened in Rainham Road. First major problems around 3am.
HILLINGDON	43	229,183	2,000+		1,200 trees replaced. Still discovering damage to trees in autumn, 1989.
HOUNSLOW	23	199,782	12,000	£1,141,000+	£5,000 a day for two months spent on clearing up.
ISLINGTON	6	159,754	1,500+	£280,000	
KEN & CHELSEA	5	138,759	800	£250,000	450 trees fall in Holland Park including rare species. Crane commandeered to lift huge tree off the Cromwell Road.
KINGSTON	15	132,411	443	£500,000	475 council homes damaged and the Guildhall, where emergency control room set up.
LAMBETH	11	245,739	10,000	£1,000,000	Sirinham Point tower block evacuated as floor collapses.
LEWISHAM	13	233,225	2,000	£1,000,000	1850 trees planted in addition to normal programme. Later estimates suggested £4.1m damage.
MERTON	15	164,912	3,000	£500,000	
NEWHAM	14	209,290	3,000	£2,000,000	4000 trees planted in two years after hurricane.
REDBRIDGE	22	225,019	3,000	£1,000,000	Tree appeal raised £30,000 in a year.
RICH UPON THAM	21	157,867	2,000	£250,000	Mayor, Councillor Martin Emerson launched tree appeal while Friends of Richmond Park received donations from far and wide.
SUTTON	17	168,407	50,000	£1,500,000	15,trees fell in Oaks Park alone where wind possibly exceeded 110mph. Firemen trapped, spent night in cottage.
SOUTHWARK	11	211,708	3,000+	£1,500,000	Buy a Tree fund launched by council in November 1987, in bid to raise £200,000. One in 10 borough trees lost.
TOWER HAMLETS	7	142,975	3,000	£2,300,000	400 trees lost in Victoria Park. Restored in Victorian style.
WALTHAM FOREST	15	215,092	2,000+	£2,000,000	Council receieved 4,500 calls for help.
WANDSWORTH	13	255,723	5,000+	£1,500,000	£50,000 worth of damage to famous pagoda in council-run Battersea Park.
WESTMINSTER	8	190,661	400		Emergency room set up at St. John's Wood. In operation for a week.
TOTAL	617.	6,696,008	300,000+	£35,000,000+	

Photograph by: Tessa Musgrave

The fourteenth National Tree Week was officially launched by the Prime Minister, Mrs Margaret Thatcher on November 28 1988 when she was guest of honour at the Chelsea Physic Garden. Here she is planting a North American paper birch, a species introduced into England in 1750. Afterwards she pledged to allocate further money to the £7 million already spent on making up for the loss of 15 million trees in the storm. Chelsea Physic Garden was founded in 1673 by the Apothecaries' Company with herbs and trees from many lands so that people could study and understand them better. The garden lost a number of notable specimens including a honey locust tree, which crashed through the roof of the house of the curator, Mr Duncan Donald.

Hyde Park lost 280 trees including those which were so badly damaged they had to be felled. Piles of logs became a familiar sight but they were soon replaced by saplings. More than 250 specimens were planted, the programme continuing into 1989.

Most of the animals at London Zoo in Regent's Park would have been terrified by the ferocity of the storm and the noise of the wind. Certainly the keepers had an anxious night, but there were no serious mishaps. The photograph above shows an 'outsider' which crashed onto empty cages. Below is the tree which grew in the compound occupied by two red pandas. Fortunately they had been moved the previous day. The row of seats on the right took the full force of the wind.

Photographs by: Zoo Operations Ltd

SORRY
ZOO CLOSED
DUE TO
STORM DAMAGE.
—
OPEN SATURDAY.

Palace loses some old friends

BUCKINGHAM Palace, one of the world's most famous residences, was built in the year of London's last great storm in 1703 by the Duke of Buckingham. In 1762 it was bought by George III and in 1825, Nash altered and remodelled it for George IV. Formerly known as Buckingham House its name was changed to Buckingham Palace but was not much used until Queen Victoria came to the throne in 1837 and has been the London home of the monarch ever since.

When the Sovereign is in residence the Royal Standard is flown day and night. At the time of the Great Storm the Queen was in Canada but was 'deeply shocked' to hear of the plight of so many people who had suffered from storm damage and the destruction of thousands of trees in the Royal Parks.

The Palace has a private garden of 40 acres and includes a lake. In the summer it is the venue for the famous garden parties. Prior to the building of the palace it was here that mulberry trees were planted by James I after 1609 to encourage the silk industry. The area was then known as the Mulberry Gardens but soon degenerated into a place of popular entertainment from 1630 to 1690. Pepys remarked that it was a 'very silly place'.

Today it is a haven of tranquillity with rich flora and fauna. On the night of the storm the Palace escaped damage but the gardens, suffered badly. Only one of the mature specimens of London plane was unscathed, ironically the tallest tree in Central London at 40 m (130 feet) high. Elsewhere, an ash had been blown down near the Hyde Park corner of the garden and sadly the stoutest known specimen of the locust tree (variety Frisia) succumbed. On an island in the lake a poplar (canadensis' Marilandica') was torn and battered.

FORECAST Date 19-10-87

	L.W.C.	Heathrow
Max. Today	17 °C	17 °C
Min. Tonight	11 °C	10 °C
Max. Tomorrow	16 °C	16 °C

TODAY'S DATE
L.W.C. Last 24 Hours

Yesterday's Max.

Last Night's Min.

D-1	Local Time	D-	MB	IN	MM	Weather
12·9	00	14·4	·	·	·	
13·	01	14·1	·	·	·	
	02	14·2	·	·	·	
	3	14·1	·	·	·	
		14·0	·	·	·	
		3·6	·	·	·	

The Home Secretary, Douglas Hurd answers questions during a press conference hastily convened at the Home Office after the capital had been hit by the storm.

Dr John Houghton, director general of the Meteorological Office holds up a chart showing the situation over Southern Britain at 5am on Friday October 16. He had been beseiged in his home by reporters and photographers asking why there had been no warning.

45

Ecclestone Square, near Victoria was one of the worst hit squares in London. Seven huge plane trees came down with eight other mature trees. However, community spirit came to the fore as this picture shows.

Photograph by: Press Association

Order and beauty has returned to Ecclestone Square. Oliver Baxter of the gardens committee is grateful to the storm for the opportunity to replant in variety.

47

The isobar map which shows lines of equal barometric pressure indicates unprecedented gradients over Southern England at 4 a.m. when the storm was raging. The lines are similar to contours drawn on a map. The closer together they are the steeper the slope. Normally there would be only two or three pressure lines. Between London and the South East coast there was an amazing difference of 12 millibars. On a map like this these lines are a good pointer to wind strengths. The wind speed exceeded 100 mph over a wide area with the most damage being recorded to the south and east of the low pressure centre. This area of low pressure reached 952 mbs a few hours earlier and was the deepest October low this century. As it moved away north-east there was a record rise of pressure.

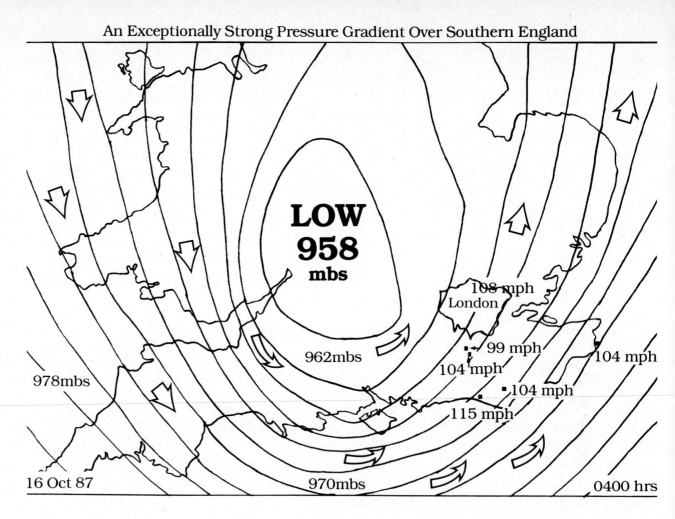

LOW
958
mbs

108 mph
London

99 mph

104 mph

104 mph

104 mph

115 mph

962mbs

978mbs

16 Oct 87

970mbs

0400 hrs

An anemogram is a record of wind speed particularly useful in the detection of individual gusts of wind which can cause so much havoc. In this example from the London Weather Centre an 82 knot (94 m.p.h.) maximum gust roared across High Holborn at 02.50hrs. G.M.T. (03.50hrs B.S.T.). Its previous highest October value was 57 knots (66 m.p.h.).

AN ANEMOGRAM FROM THE LONDON WEATHER CENTRE 15th/16th OCTOBER 1987

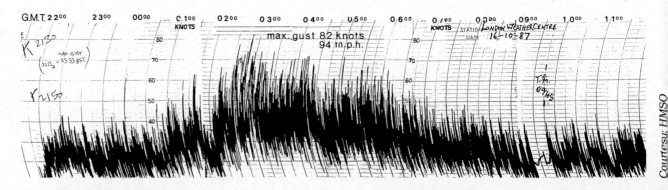

max. gust 82 knots
94 m.p.h.

Courtesy: HMSO

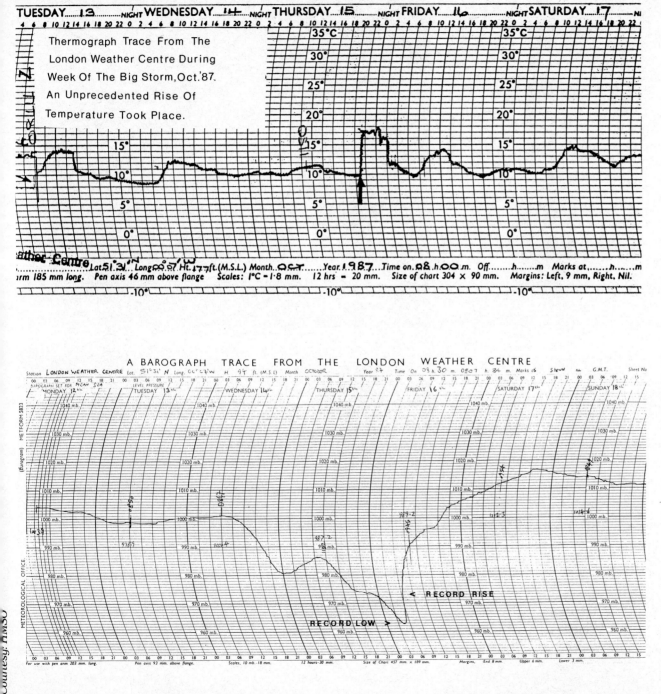

A BAROGRAPH TRACE FROM THE LONDON WEATHER CENTRE

A burst of summerlike warmth heralded the start of London's worst storm since 1703. The arrow shows that around 2100 hours a normal October night was transformed by an invasion of sub-tropical air forced north-eastwards by the developing storm. The temperature rise of more than 7c (13f) in less than half an hour is without parallel and at Heathrow to the west and Coulsdon to the south near Croydon there were similar remarkable surges of heat recorded.

A barograph trace is a continuous record of air-pressure values, and the exceptional nature of the Great Storm is clearly shown on this chart from the London Weather Centre. The canyon-like trough down to 963 millibars and the equally impressive rise exceeded anything previously recorded in October.

Time flies in Blackheath

TIME literally flew in Blackheath when the clock blew off St. John's Church and landed on a path in front of the buiding. Its black and gold numbers glistened in the sunshine next morning when it was discovered by the clock-winder, Mr Angus Ogilvie. The church spire was severely damaged and the lead ridge capping was stripped off along the whole length of the roof of the church. In the months following the storm £80,000 was spent on renovating the spire and the crumpled clock was repaired, regilded and replaced.

Photographs by: Charles H. Jones

Photograph by: Fern Flunn

Young Tess Copping from Blackheath gets to grips with the oldest living tree in London, a horse chestnut in Greenwich Park planted in 1684. Unlike many of the younger trees in the park it survived the storm, although losing some branches. However, at 305 years old, it is still bearing chestnuts.

The storm really caused a song and dance in Greenwich, but these energetic children from the Marjorie Hawkins School of Irish Dancing quickly sprang into action and raised £100 for new trees. They presented their cheque to the mayor, John Austin Walker, whose tree appeal hit the £500 mark just two weeks after the storm. Pictured from left to right with the mayor are Sinead Bloomfield, Nyrene O'Halloran, Michelle Foran, Jemma Letch, Emmet McGoran, Melissa Wall and Claire Bentley.

Greenwich is one of the greenest boroughs in London and it suffered terrible damage. 1,800 street trees and 10,000 park and woodland trees were destroyed including many precious oaks and sweet chestnuts which were more than 100 years old. This chaotic scene is the Greenwich High Road.

The 53 bus edges past debris at the Royal Standard, Blackheath on the morning of the storm. It was one of the few London buses to run that day. For one driver, though, the worst hurricane to hit Britain in living memory was not going to deter him. Brian Ward from Holloway found his N93 route strewn with obstacles, but he steered his way through, picking up passengers whenever he felt they needed a lift. Mr P.R. Evans of Richmond wrote to the London Evening Standard, praising his efforts. Mr Evans had found no trains running from Richmond on either the overground or Underground services. Suddenly, driver Ward stopped the bus and asked if he needed a lift. He picked up 20 other passengers who were also looking lost and confused, took detours to avoid debris and trees, and dropped Mr Evans at his office door in Fleet Street.

An unexpected bank holiday

THE City was like a ghost-town on Friday morning with the normal hectic rush-hour replaced by a few intrepid path-finders who had braved countless obstacles and pioneered new routes on their normally routine journey to the office.

One place which felt the effects of the storm was the London Stock Exchange which had the air of numbed disbelief that the weather could shut down an institution; that it could penetrate right to the heart of the City. But shut down it did as dealing screens went blank due to power failure and key telephone exchanges went out of action. The Exchange suspended equity trading and halted foreign dealings.

It was the quietest day in living memory for those dealers who made it to their desks. Even the January blizzards which isolated whole towns in Kent and Essex did not grind London to a halt. Friday October 16 1987 was, according to one broker, much quieter than Christmas Eve.

Not far away the Bank of England was sharing a similar fate; no power or communications led to a halt of buying and selling and there were no settlements that day. In effect a Bank Holiday!

What followed on the Monday and Tuesday was not the crash of falling trees but a storm of a different kind, a slump of 22 per cent on the FTSE Index. Such unprecedented volatility brought 100,000 transactions a day with a value of £3.5 billion on the 20th alone.

Though there is no suggestion that the storm precipitated Black Monday, which was on a worldwide scale affecting all financial markets, the lull in trading on the Friday could have exacerbated the number of transactions following the week-end. Whatever the causes the City will never forget October '87, Storm or Crash!

Flying Saucer

Anneliese Cashmore moved out of her basement flat in Drayton Gardens, South Kensington while it was being redecorated — and it was just as well she did. A huge metal water tank lid was lifted from the roof of the six-storey block opposite and sent spinning through the air, demolishing part of a fence at street level. The ornamental wrought iron fence then speared the basement windows in the room where Anneliese might have been sitting. She now believes in flying saucers.

A scrapyard behind advertisement hoardings is revealed by this fallen tree. In the background is Deptford Power Station.

Photograph by: Sass Tuffin

54

Scaffolding was blown down across the City of London, disrupting traffic and closing many roads. In this picture debris is scattered far and wide across Norton Folgate, just north of Liverpool Street Station.

The Great Tempest of 1703 in London

IT was in the second year of Queen Anne's reign that London was struck by a violent storm that left the city broken and battered. Whole buildings were razed to the ground, thousands of trees felled; boats on the Thames smashed and splintered but worst of all was the toll of death and injury and the hardships suffered by those who endured broken homes in an English winter.

The writer Daniel Defoe, of Robinson Crusoe fame, and a keen weather watcher, experienced the sheer terror of that storm and published a documentary account with the graphic title: "The Storm or a Collection of The Most Remarkable Casualties and Disasters which happened in the late Dreadful Tempest both by Sea and Land".

From Defoe's description and the many reports sent to him, including one from Upminster compiled by the Reverend Derham, we can guess that an intense area of low pressure crossed the Midlands and out into the North Sea. Defoe's barometer was reading so low he thought that children had been playing with it.

The 1703 storm was preceded by a week or so of disturbed weather. Defoe himself was nearly killed by a house which collapsed on the evening of November 24 when London was hit by terrible squalls of rain. On the 25th the City was beset by thunder and hail storms, and it was with no surprise to Londoners that the next day dawned windy and continued so all day.

That night Defoe awoke at midnight as a steadily rising wind shrieked and moaned around his house. By two o'clock few people were unaware of the increasing frenzy of the wind. Conditions outside became so bad that Defoe wrote "nobody durst quit their tottering habitations for it was worse without". The wind tore through the streets and increased to such a pitch that many thought the end of the world was nigh. Just before daybreak the storm reached its climax of destruction. According to Defoe nothing would have survived if it had continued much longer.

When day break came London was a changed city with its streets choked with rubble from fallen masonry, masses of tiles stripped from roofs and strewn everywhere some being embedded several inches into the ground. Ships at anchor on the Thames were blown from their moorings and piled together between Bell Wharf and Limehouse in a manner described as 'incredible and impossible'. Nobody could believe the hundreth part they saw".

Countless chimney stacks fell in the storm and Defoe mentioned Cambray House near Islington belonging to the Earl of Northampton which lost 13, and he knew of 20 houses totally demolished.

One consequence of the tempest was that the price of tiles escalated so much that many houses were left open to the elements or covered by wooden planking.

There were reports of death and injury from all over the city. A woman was killed near St. James's Palace; a distiller in Dukes Street was buried by a roof collapse, which killed the maid as well, but his wife survived. In Fetter lane a Mr Dyer was fatally struck by a chimney stack and so were two boys in Cross Street, Hatton Garden and a woman in Jewin Street who foolishly ventured out on to the storm-lashed streets where it was said that tiles were blown 40 yards and driven eight inches into the ground. Two more people died in Aldersgate Street when a house collapsed.

Many householders were huddled in ground floor rooms fearing the worst while others remained in their beds. In Threadneedle Street a Mr Simpson was roused from his sleep and pleaded with to rise from his bed but unfortunately took no heed of the warning and within minutes was buried under tons of rubble. Another man, a carpenter, in WhitecrossStreet was crushed by a similar fall of debris. This same fate befell the Bishop of Wells who was struck by a falling chimney stack while asleep in bed. In London alone 21 people were killed. Near Moorfields a whole row of houses was levelled, though no details of casualties are known.

From all over London there were reports of damage to buildings. At Greenwich Park some 500 yards of wall was destroyed. A part of her Majesty's Palace caved in with such a terrible noise as "very much alarmed the whole household".

The lead on the roof of Westminster Abbey was "rolled up like parchment and blown clear of the building". The ferocious winds battered London's churches. The top of St Mary Aldernay was blown off and sent crashing on to the roof. St Mary Overies, St Michael and St Sepulchres all succumbed to the forces of nature.

Many trees were blown down, 70 at Moorfields, 100 at St. James's Park and 200 at Whitmoor House. Across Southern England more than 450 parks and groves were damaged, 400 windmills destroyed and 800 houses demolished.

One of the most dramatic stories from 1703 was the loss of the Eddystone Lighthouse. The builder Winstanley had realised in 1698 that it needed to be raised higher and strengthened and this was duly carried out.

In order to check the improvements he set out for the reef on the Thursday. When the seas subsided after the storm there was no trace of him, his workmen or the keepers and the lighthouse was obliterated.

Devastation on water was not confined to the seas. The damage to shipping along the Thames defied description. Defoe saw 700 ships between Shadwell and Limehouse "most crushed together", one boat rammed up and over the other and concertinaed in "a grotesque manner". Some 500 wherries were lost and 60 sunk between London Bridge and Hammersmith. Two watermen were drowned at Blackfriars endeavouring to save their boat and a boat capsized near Fulham killing five persons.

Altogether the cost of the Storm in London alone was put at £2 million, an astronomic figure for the early 18th century. But mercifully in the words of one witness there were some 'remarkable preservations'.

A milk-maid who ventured out in the teeth of the gale was blown into a pond and after struggling furiously only just managed to avoid being drowned. Perhaps the most miraculous deliverance took place at St Martins Lane where at three in the morning a furious gust blew down a stack of chimneys onto the residence of Mr Robert Richards an apothecary at the sign of the Unicorn and Capt. Theodore Collier and his family. There were 17 people in the house as the chimney smashed its way to the ground floor.

A footman changed rooms just before his garret collapsed. A baby, nurse and maid were in the room below and were swept down three stories to the kitchen. Amazingly the child was found unharmed hanging in curtains having fallen through two floors; the other two sustaining only slight bruises. Capt. Collier and his wife were buried under masonry but were pulled out unhurt. The Richards family escaped into the street but poor Mrs. Richards and her little boy found the house collapsing on top of them. After scrambling from the wreckage with no more than a bruised foot she fetched help and they feverishly sought the child in the rubble and to their astonishment they located the cradle and pulled out the baby alive and well.

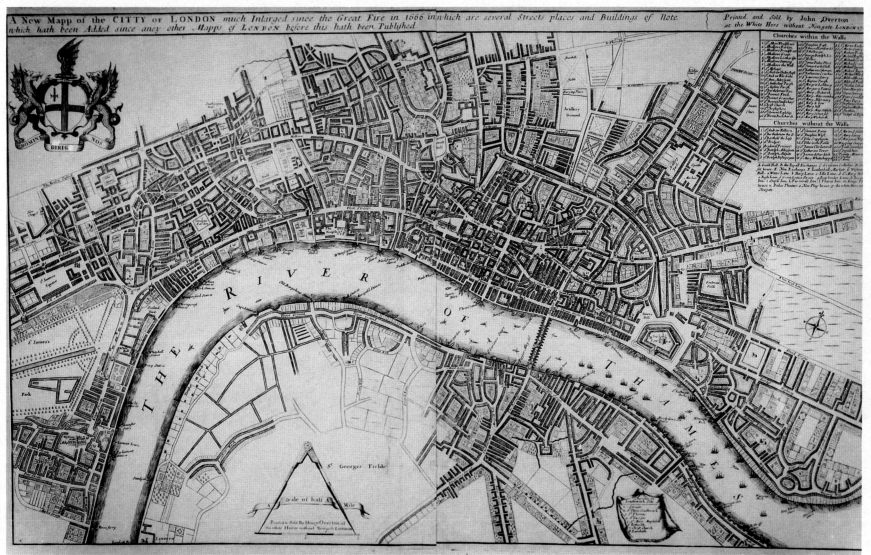

A New Mapp of the CITTY of LONDON much Inlarged since the Great Fire in 1666 in which are several Streets places and Buildings of Note which hath been Added since aney other Mapps of LONDON before this hath been Publyshed.

Printed and Sold by John Overton at the White Hors without Newgate LONDON

LONDON IN 1706

LONDON in the reign of Queen Anne was small indeed compared to the sprawling metropolis of the twentieth century. Much of what is now Greater London was countryside and far removed from the hustle and bustle of city life. The City itself had spread out beyond the London Wall but Westminster was still a rural retreat with an aptly named Orchard Street. The City was largely rebuilt after the Great Fire in 1666, a factor which was instrumental in saving it from even worse damage during the 1703 storm. New buildings were largely brick-built and more substantial than the previous wooden structures. The map printed in 1706 shows the multi-arched London Bridge as the only path-way across the Thames, something inconceivable for modern London. The narrow arches helped in the icing-over of the river during severe winters and the creation of the famous Frost Fairs.

57

A Storm Proclamation Commanded by Her Majesty Queen Anne January 1704

Courtesy of Guildhall Library

"WHEREAS, by the late most terrible and dreadful Storms of Wind with which it hath pleased Almighty God to afflict the greatest part of this our kingdom, on Friday and Saturday, the twenty sixth and twenty seventh day of November last some of our Ships of War and many ships of our loving subjects have been destroyed and lost at sea, and great numbers of our subjects, serving on board the same have perished, and many houses and other buildings of our good subjects have been either wholly thrown down and demolished or very much damnified and defaced, and thereby several persons have been killed, and many Stacks of Corn and Hay thrown down and scattered abroad, to the great damage and impoverishment of many others, especially the poorer sort and great numbers of timber and other trees have by the said Storm been torn up by the roots in many parts of this our said Kingdom; a Calamity of this sort so dreadful and astonishing, that the like hath not been seen or felt in the memory of any person living in this our Kingdom, and which loudly calls for the deepest and most solemn humiliation of us and our people; therefore out of a deep and pious sense of what we and all our people have suffered by this said dreadful Wind and Storm (which we most humbly acknowledge to be a token of the Divine displeasure, and this it was the infinite mercy of God that we and our people were not thereby wholly destroyed), we have resolved and do hereby command, that a General Public Fast be observed."

This public fast was accordingly observed throughout England, on January 19, 1704.

The Queen was in Canada when the storm struck England. She sent her condolences to the families of those who lost their lives and, on her return, planted a tree in Kensington Gardens.

Photograph by Royal Parks staff

Funny weather isn't it?

LONDON'S ability to laugh at itself in adversity is world renowned and the great storm provided enough anecdotal ammunition to keep pubs, clubs, offices and factories rocking with laughter for some weeks. In fact, hurricane stories, like the event itself have become part of London's folklore.

The unfortunate Michael Fish bore the brunt of the capital's mirth following his chance remark that there wasn't a hurricane on its way. He did say there would be strong winds and he did say there was a vicious-looking area of low-pressure on our doorsteps. When London awoke in the dark to find itself paralysed they looked for a scapegoat and the media, cruelly, singled out the unfortunate Mr Fish.

Thousands of Londoners slept through the storm completely unaware of the drama of the night. When they were roused from their slumbers they found that the bedside light wouldn't work. One hotel porter was asked politely to mend a fuse. "Sir", he said firmly, "it's not your table lamp. It's the whole of southern England!"

Before the storm tree surgeons arrived at Biggin Hill Airport, Bromley to examine dangerous trees. They marked them with a big yellow cross and ordered them to be felled. Then came the hurricane which turned aeroplanes upside down. The only trees standing on the airfield all had a big yellow cross marked on them!

Outside the capital, Rambo, an oversexed ram was delighted when the gale destroyed the fence protecting a herd of pedigree sheep. At the height of the storm he wandered into the woolly compound for a night of wild passion much to the owner's displeasure.

A man wandered outside of his London flat to see what the noise was all about. He was wearing his rather old but warm and comfortable heavy woollen dressing gown. In the garden a gust of wind blew up his legs, picked him up and sent him spiralling into the air. He actually parachuted down to earth slowly — his dressing gown billowing above his head.

One busy day just after the storm a loss adjuster, investigating a routine claim, visited a house in North London, noted the damage and was shown to a greenhouse in the rear garden. A brief examination revealed only two broken panes and the adjuster asked whether an estimate had been obtained for repair. "I don't know", replied the insured. "It's not my greenhouse. I found it here on the morning of October 16.

A man was asleep on the top floor of a three-storey building when he was awoken by the chimney crashing through the roof, through his bedroom, through the floor below and eventually to the basement. The man, waking quickly from a deep sleep, jumped out of bed. If he had jumped to the right he would have followed the chimney all the way to the basement. But he jumped to the left.

Lord Marshall chairman of the Central Electricity Generating Board said after the storm: "Everyone has been congratulating me on my influence with the Almighty for laying on the hurricane as a demonstration of our efficiency.

A 25 foot high fibre-glass strawberry was blown away from outside Hewitts Farm in Court Road, Orpington.

Alasdair McDonald was walking along West India Dock Road when a lady in front of him narrowly missed being killed by a sheet of corrugated steel. Chaos was all around. "Blowy this morning isn't it" she said.

Oliver Baxter of Ecclestone Square, London, had fought hard to have some plane trees removed, . . . they shaded his roses. The storm removed seven planes and now his roses are flourishing.

One person from Tooting was annoyed to find a neighbour had pinched his parking spot when he arrived home from work. But the next morning when he looked out, his rancour turned to mirth. A tree had flattened the car.

Independent Radio News lost both power and telephones and broadcast studio reports from the engineers control room using a single microphone passed from hand to hand.

A deck-chair was precariously perched on top of a bush in St. James Park, whilst a pot plant landed on a traffic island.

On the morning after the storm a man was seen brewing up a cup of tea on a gas stove. He worked in the electricity showroom.

A husband left home to go on a business trip on October 15. His wife's lover arrived soon after his departure. The storm blew down trees in the drive trapping the lover's car. October 16th worried husband immediately returns home to wife to find — no lover but one very incriminating car in the drive!

Royal Parks lose 5,000 trees

THE Tree Council was founded in 1973 as a government sponsored body to promote a tree planting campaign with the slogan "plant a tree in '73". Now it has charity status.

One of the Council's schemes is National Tree Week and since the storm these have become especially important, for the loss of trees amounted to 15 million in just a few hours. In London itself a quarter of a million were destroyed, a sad blow to the urban dweller. These included nearly 5,000 in the Royal Parks and 100 damaged or felled in the heart of the City.

One of the most successful replanting events in the London area during tree week was at Oaks Park, Sutton, where the savage winds had pole-axed thousands of trees. Through the British Trust for Conservation Volunteers, 500 people were mustered on a cold and frosty Sunday morning in late November 1988 to plant 500 trees.

Help was certainly needed for the scale of damage could be judged by the fact that an extra £2.75 million was granted to the Countryside Commission to help repair the landscape, administered by a special unit called Task-Force Trees. Yet when local authorities catalogued their destruction and put in a bid for funds the total amount came to a staggering £8·4 million.

Londoners' responded well to the variety of tree-fund appeals including those by local councils. Redbridge raised £30,000. Glaxo-Pharmaceuticals donated £5,500 to the Borough of Ealing enough to replace 250 trees, and the Royal Family took part in a number of events. The Queen planted an oak at Runnymede as part of National Tree Week. The Prince of Wales planted a tree in Hyde Park to launch his Royal Parks Appeal. The Princess of Wales visited Kensington Gardens in February 1988 and planted a mature oak near the Orangery. It was here that some of the worst devastation of all occurred with the complete destruction of Jubilee Avenue.

A conference organised by the Tree Council entitled 'After the Storm — One Year On' was told it would take many years for the landscape to recover. However the audience also heard that it was not all doom and gloom for here was a golden opportunity to replan and improve our environment. Many tree's root systems and patterns of growth could now be studied and the most suitable type of tree selected for replanting. Perhaps the most beneficial aspect was the new-found awareness among the public that trees are not eternal. They need care and attention. Children in particular have become more sensitive to their surroundings and if this attitude continues it bodes well for the future.

Photograph by Richmond and Twickenham Times

A white magnolia planted by the wife of the Japanese Prime Minister at Kew Gardens marked Japan's donation of £8,000 to the Kew hurricane fund. Madame Laoko Takeshita dug in the magnolia Kobus, native to Japan. It bears small white flowers.

Photograph by: Daily Mail, Solo.

Ashley Stevenson of the Royal Parks contemplates the task ahead at Greenwich Park.

61

A crisis in the East End

STAFF at East London's 999 fire control room at Romford Road, Stratford, will never forget "the night they thought The Bomb had dropped!"

All was quiet until the small hours when South London's control room asked East London if they were getting calls about trees down. The answer was no, but it was the signal of terrible things to come.

Just before 3am the first distress calls flashed up, reporting trees falling and slates skeltering down roofs. Within minutes all hell broke loose. The switchboard was alight with calls; so many that people had to wait in queues before they could be answered. The situation was so grim, a state of emergency was declared. Controller Steve Lashmar recalled: "We were more than stretched. We were overwhelmed".

Fire engines themselves were becoming trapped by trees, and the radio system was fading away. On an emergency standby radio, officers were battling to get their urgent messages to control. A faint voice drowned out by dozens of distorted messages, pleaded for more assistance. It came from the crew of an engine sent out to a fallen tree, which, by chance, had spotted a factory on fire in Abbey Road, Barking. They wanted three more machines. Only one could be spared.

Scores of frightened old ladies rang up — some wanting to hear a reassuring voice. One of them called to say her power had gone off, and at that moment, the control room was plunged into darkness. Area controller Mick Warwick shouted out an order for everyone to stay still. Within seconds an emergency generator had fired up.

The North East area staff team arrived from Poplar, providing the best help available — mugs of tea. Up until then, there was no time to put the kettle on.

Staff worked 20 hour shifts dealing as quickly and as politely as possible with the public. Controller Janice Minshall did not want to go home. She felt as if a bomb had dropped. When she did leave, her ears throbbing through having worn a headset for so long, she glanced at the outside world in a trance and thought to herself: "There are no trees".

By midnight on Friday October 16, the Stratford control had received 1,009 storm calls — and answered 640 of them. That wasn't the end of the problem. Eastenders jammed the switchboard in the days that followed, pleading for assistance as rainwater poured in through gaping holes in roofs and ceilings.

Photograph by Mark Davison

Fire Brigade controllers Janice Minshall and Steve Lashmar recalling the events in the East End 999 nerve centre.

Families evacuated

A tower block on the Nightingale Estate in Lower Clapton was swaying in the wind so residents were evacuated. They took refuge in Hackney police station.

Fifty families were evacuated in Stoke Newington when a gas main was fractured by a fallen tree. Another family were trapped in a car by a fallen tree on the Old Ford Road. They were rescued by council staff.

London Weekend Television crews filming an episode of London's Burning at Dockhead fire station had to pack up because of the noise. They went ahead with their weekly draw and donated £80 to the families of two firemen killed in Dorset when a tree fell on their fire engine. Nationwide 19 people lost their lives.

This huge crane which can lift five tonnes of cargo was built for the Port of London Authority in 1961. It normally moves along a track like a giant railway train but it toppled over sideways at the Central Dock, Tilbury during the storm. The crane was sent for scrap following the incident.

The wind blew hot and cold in Mr Athansi Andrew's hair-styling salon with such force that nothing was left standing. The shop had stood for 25 years in Green Street, Upton Park and Mr Andrews was dumbfounded when he arrived in the morning to find windows and walls blown down.

Photograph by: Guardian and Gazette Newspapers

The weather provided a spectacle of its own early on Friday morning but not one that pleased the owner of Jimmy Fossett's Circus on Chingford Plain. It caused an estimated £10,000 worth of damage, the Big-Top being torn to shreds. Amazingly the show did go on the following day in a make shift tent.

65

List of priorities

AFTER hurried consultations in the dead of night, Waltham Forest Borough Council put its Natural Disaster Emergency Plan into operation and immediately devised a list of priorities. One was to remove a tree which was blocking the road to the ambulance station and another was to clear the way to Whipps Cross Hospital.

More than 4,500 calls for help were received by the council. This included a distress call from an elderly lady who was trapped in her home by a fallen tree.

British Rail suspended all services in the borough and the Central Line of the Underground between Epping and Ongar was out of action all day.

A few days after the big wind storm came the big rain storm. More than 25mm fell in the north-east of London and the fire brigade received 527 flood calls. The midnight emergency control was re-established and received many calls from the occupants of flooded homes where rainwater had cascaded through damaged roofs.

More than 40,000 Waltham Forest schoolchildren had a day off school. Many were away for over a week.

Oblivious tramp

YORKIE the tramp who lived in a bus shelter at Lissenden Gardens, Gospel Oak, had a narrow escape when a tree fell, missing him by inches. He slept on regardless, and on waking at 9 a.m. asked a policeman who had been chopping down the trees in the night.

Photograph by: Guardian and Gazette Newspapers

Five cars in Oliver Close car park were crushed when an entire wall fell out at Cross Point Motors, Oliver Road, Leyton. The spray booths in the factory and three vehicles were also damaged. Repairs exceeded £200,000.

Almost deserted

THERE was an air of unreality on the streets of Newham on the Friday morning. Every machine and every fireman from the borough fire service were in action and all the schools were closed. The Gospel Oak to Barking railway line was also closed and so were all the parks. The usually busy streets were almost deserted.

Most of the lime and plane trees planted in Newham, because they were tolerant to smogs came down in the storm. This has enabled the borough to plant a greater variety of species which will survive in the less polluted air. One of the first to be planted was a pillar crab (malus tschonoskii) in Lucas Avenue, Plaistow.

THE River Thames turned into a tempestuous sea, tearing barges from their moorings and hurling them into the middle of the river, causing a danger to navigation. London Phoenix the capital's fire boat was alerted to a string of boats, tied to each other, which were adrift. The crew recalled 'mammoth waves in the pitch dark'; an eerie experience.

Photograph by Newham and Dockland Recorder.

When repairs are being carried out on your house the last thing you want is the worst storm for nearly 300 years to blast through it and do its own alterations. When workmen returned to the site in Coleridge Avenue, Manor Park, they found a chaotic heap of scaffolding and broken tiles.

Leafy Redbridge

THE leafy borough of Redbridge lost more than 1,000 trees from its streets. A particularly sad loss was the 400-year-old yew at St. Mary's Church, South Woodford.

THE roof of Barking bus garage was ripped open. Similar dramas occurred at Nightingale School, South Woodford and Uphall School, Ilford.

WHEN a chimney in Tennyson Avenue, Wanstead crashed through the roof it miraculously hit the water tank. Mr Thomas who was asleep in his bedroom at the time, was showered with water rather than masonry. The wind then tore his house apart leaving gaping holes in the roof and smashing walls in the bedroom and bathroom.

ALL schools in Redbridge were closed on the Friday. 60 trees had fallen onto the Epping to Ongar section of the Central Line.

THE ravaged Redbridge landscape prompted both the council and public to organise a programme of replanting and money-raising. A Tree Appeal Fund raised, in little over a year, £30,000 more than any other London borough. Some of the money came from re-cycled paper, itself a product of trees, and the enthusiasm was so great that the replanting continued into 1989.

Victoria Park, Hackney lost hundreds of trees. Here are some more victims.

VICTORIA Park was created by public demand in 1845 after a petition signed by 30,000 East-Enders was presented to Queen Victoria. Increasing urbanisation had meant that there was scant room for a healthy and recreational open space. They did not go unheeded and York House was sold and land acquired. James Pennethorne, the creator of Battersea Park designed this new one called Victoria Park. In recent years Victoria Park's 280 acres has still enjoyed its role as the East End's favourite beauty spot with its lakes, flower beds and herds of deer. The morning of the October 16 revealed utter mayhem. Some 403 trees lay pole-axed with another 200 damaged. The state of the trees made conditions so dangerous that the park gates were welded shut to prevent the public from entering. Great efforts were made by the staff to clear the debris and to restore the area to its former glory. This action was aided by £5000 raised from the Little Acorns appeal and an £8000 grant from the Countryside Commission. More than 530 trees have been replanted and a specialist contractor has been brought in to catalogue the ages, types and health of all the remaining trees. The park has now been listed by English Heritage as one of historical importance.

An emergency round every corner

THE men and women of the London Fire Brigade do not only fight fires. They rescue people and animals who are trapped. They attend road accidents, often cutting mangled bodies out of mangled cars. They stand by at airports and hospitals. And they pump out flooded homes.

On October 16, 1987 the London Fire Brigade dealt with all these emergencies and many, many more. Four thousand calls were received in just a few hours creating a pressure that was without precedent in peacetime. There are 6,800 firefighters in London's 114 stations. Together they covered 620 miles and displayed their capacity for intense and sustained effort.

There was an emergency around almost every corner but these skilled technicians dealt with them all, shrugged of burns and lacerations as a routine part of the job, and responded at top speed, regardless of conditions.

Calls to fallen trees became routine but there were many other dramatic incidents. At Beckenham, a newspaper boy crushed under a fallen tree, was rescued. In Islington, North London, a man was trapped by falling debris in the basement of a house. He was released by firemen after an emergency medical team gave him first aid.

One of the most spectacular events concerned the tower block at Kennington, South London which started to crumble several floors up. The Brigade evacuated 84 families.

Fire calls received priority and were attended in the normal manner, with requests for special services dealt with on a priority basis of risk to life, assistance to hospitals, the elderly and infirm. Many requests were received for tree felling, and taking into account risks to life and property, were dealt with when resources were available. A procedure was rapdily devised in which station commanders investigated all calls to decide the degree of urgency.

The considerable problems were made worse at 4.23 am when a power cut blacked out all three mobilising controls and the central operations room at Lambeth HQ. Generators came into operation, but teleprinter links to fire stations were not working in all but one of the control rooms, so radio telephones had to be used for several hours until the main electricity was restored.

The Lambeth HQ opened a special incident room to ease pressure on the three mobilising controls by taking over many of the non-emergency tasks, including liaising with local councils and dealing with hundreds of media enquiries.

Photograph by John Powell

Firemen at Morden in South London remove a dangerous chimney stack.

London Fire Brigade received 4,063 distress calls between midnight on Thursday October 15 to midnight on the Friday — 10 times more than normal. Here a fireman attends to a car crushed by a tree in Northfields, Ealing W13.

Improved vistas from Hampstead Heath

MANY people mourned the loss of so many fine trees on Hampstead Heath. Nature's power had punched huge holes in the woodland and opened up so many amazing vistas that after a while the same people began to appreciate what the storm had achieved. One improved view across London is from Parliament Hill, 319 feet above sea level.

Historian Albert Gunther wrote this about Hampstead Heath after the storm. "Whereas Hampstead's Lime Avenue offers an extraordinary scene of desolation with trunks lying pell-mell across the road, the coach-age oaks still stand solitary and proud in a line along the wreckage. Most sadly, one of the severest of the hurricane's blasts hit the forest plateau west of Kenwood Gate. There half a dozen magnificent oaks lie prostrate across the track, one having taken its vengeance on a beech by landing its branch on it".

It was estimated that 28,000 trees fell in the borough of Camden with more than 1,000 toppling in streets and parks. Seventy roads were blocked. Hampstead Heath was used as a massive timber store and about 2,000 tonnes of wood were eventually transported to and from the store at a cost of £200,000.

The long established newspaper, The Hampstead and Highgate Express — affectionately known as "The Ham and High" — thought the wind had done amazingly well.

It stated: "Too many trees have been planted on the Heath in recent years and the gale force winds played a positive part in removing some, especially on the West Heath, and in creating vistas that had been lost. The situation presents an opportunity to prepare a comprehensive tree policy for the Heath's future".

In Red Lion Square, Holborn, the statue of veteran socialist politician and peace campaigner, Lord Brockway was knocked down and badly disfigured.

Gerald Ronson of Winnington Road, Hampstead Garden Suburb was one of the heroes of the night. he rescued an office worker who was trapped under a collapsed wall in Baker Street.

In Rosecroft Avenue, residents of a block of 10 flats were evacuated at 7 a.m. on the Friday morning when a tree tore up a gas main causing an additional hazard.

An explosion in the population of stag beetles on Hampstead Heath was blamed on the storm. Author and naturalist John Hillaby found 10 different specimens in such places as Kenwood, Flask Walk and Frognal Lane and said there was so much lying timber rotting away in the copses that the beetles had found the perfect habitat. The discovery has been logged by the Natural History Museum. John Hillaby is pictured above with a lesser stag beetle (dorcus parallel-pipedus).

An explosion in the population of stag beetles has occurred at Hampsted Heath because of so much lying timber rotting away in the copses. Picture shows insect expert, John Hillaby with a lesser stag beetle which has found the perfect habitat. John, an author and naturalist, has found many different specimens of the beetle. Other insects also thrive.

Photograph by: Hampstead Highgate Express

THIS AVENUE WAS REPLANTED
IN NOVEMBER 1988 TO REPLACE TREES
DESTROYED BY A HURRICANE
DURING THE NIGHT OF 15/16 OCTOBER 1987
TREES DONATED BY
THE HEATH & OLD HAMPSTEAD SOCIETY
THE FRANKLIN COLE FOUNDATION
TASK FORCE TREES & ERIC WOODS, ESQ.

LONDON RESIDUARY BODY

Photographs by: Fern Flynn

Hampsteads Heath's famous Lime Avenue is restored to much of its former beauty, young trees replacing the fallen. A plaque commemorates the storm and the help given in the restoration.

More than 600 trees were brought down on London Underground tracks. Three huge poplars fell at Morden station and 60 trees fell on the Epping-Ongar line which was closed for several days. Other problem lines were the Metropolitan between Rickmansworth and Chesham and the Central between Leytonstone and Debden, and at Sudbury and Upminster. This picture shows a Piccadilly line train in Middlesex edging past a fallen tree which had just been cut back by London Underground "permanent way vegetation control staff".

The problem facing this milkman in Conway Crescent, Perivale, was more than pint size but despite many obstacles such as this, deliveries were still made. Such is the determination of the staff of Unigate Dairies, Wembley.

Photograph by: Stanmore Observer

Photographs by: Mark Davison

Two pictures taken from the same spot in Old Church Lane, Stanmore.
On Friday October 16, 1987 residents struggled to get out of their front doors. today it is back to normal — minus the trees.

There was no discrimination. Even the friendly tree surgeon had his truck damaged at Torrington Park, North Finchley.

Photographs by: Gareth Beard, Wembley Observer

The BMX boys meet an obstacle in Preston Road, Wembley.

THE RIGHT HONOURABLE THE LORD MAYOR

SIR CHRISTOPHER COLLETT GBE MA DSc

THE MANSION HOUSE LONDON EC4N 8BH
TELEPHONE 01-626 2500

      Bob Ogley's previous book,
"In the Wake of the Hurricane", was a piece
of highly commendable instant local history
that captured the public imagination and
became a best seller in its national edition.

      The series of hurricane books which
Froglets Publications have so far produced
have raised helpful amounts of money for a
variety of charities, and that is why I am
delighted to be associated with this latest
publication on the storm of October 1987,
and how it affected London the capital City,
which this year celebrates the 800th anniversary
of the foundation of its Mayoralty.

      I am sure that like its predecessors
this book will provide a remarkable record
of an event which changed the face of Britain
and gave all of us a fresh awareness of the
power of nature.

LORD MAYOR

800th ANNIVERSARY OF THE MAYORALTY
1189-1989

Life must go on and there are groceries to get in for the weekend. A defiant resident of Hatch End ignores the devastation on the Uxbridge Road.

Ealing fills the gaps

EALING Borough Council launched a major tree appeal which was called "Fill The Gaps". The campaign encouraged residents to adopt a tree and commemorate it to somebody special. By April 1, 1989 5,400 replacement trees had been planted.

EIGHTY out of 90 schools in the borough of Ealing reported either structural damage or trees down in the grounds. Dormers Wells High lost part of the kitchen roof, at Downe Manor First and Middle a large tree fell on a classroom and at Ealing College, Greenwood First and Middle and Our Lady of Visitation there was extensive damage.

COFFIN bearers in Bernard Road, Ealing had to pick their way through trees as one family proceeded with the funeral of a loved one. Elsewhere in the borough, wartime shrapnel was found embedded in trees and this timber could not be sold to merchants.

FOR more than a century, Ealing was considered to be the capital's most sylvan borough. Its tree-lined streets and areas of parkland led to the accolade Queen of The Suburbs. A bruised and battered "queen" lost 5,000 trees but the former glory will soon return.

Photograph by Middlesex Chronicle

The cars have been abandoned but an intrepid cyclist finds a way round this fallen tree. This is Teddington in the borough of Richmond-upon-Thames where 2,000 trees fell.

Storm gods of Tooting

SCULPTOR Mark Folds created several monuments out of storm-damaged trees on Tooting Common, because he was so devastated at the loss.

One of the oak statues which depicted a man holding an old tree and a young sapling was carved near to where Wandsworth Council held a tree planting ceremony in December 1987, in the presence of TV stars Nerys Hughes and Susannah York and Mayor of Wandsworth Councillor Duncan Hawkins.

Sadly, vandals struck within days. One of the sculptures had its arm snapped off and the other lost both arms and was found lying on the ground. Another was found dumped in the garden of a Clapham public house to the astonishment of the landlord. But Mark, then aged 24, was determined to restore his work.

In the summer of 1989, the Storm Gods stood proud once again, and were admired by the hundreds of Tooting and Balham residents whose favourite open space has been provided with many new young trees.

TEENAGER, Kelly Ford had an amazing escape when a tree fell on his house at Bexleyheath. "It was about 4am when the storm was at its worst. I was lying on my back and I heard a loud snapping noise which woke me. Then I saw bricks coming down from the ceiling. I got my head in the pillow as it all caved in on top of me."

His frantic father. Tony thought Kelly was dead when he rushed into the room. He couldn't hear him breathing. There was dust and debris everywhere. Then he heard him moaning and with his bare hands pulled everything off him.

Plumstead Common where many splendid trees were lost. This was taken from the Old Mill Road on the morning after.

Photograph by Lianne Sutton

This is Bushy Park which is close to Hampton Court. Together the two royal parks lost an estimated 2,000 trees.

London's plane trees showed little resistance to the wind. This one crushed a red Mazda in King Alfred Avenue, Catford.

Photograph by D.G. Wallis.

Comprehensive destruction at Monks Orchard Road, Shirley in the borough of Croydon.

There were two fatalities in London on the night of the storm and one was in Lincoln's Inn Fields where this picture was taken. Terrence Marrin was killed when he was hit by a plane tree.

The wind forced this street light to kiss the centre of the road. This is the Bayswater Road, Hyde Park.

Hundreds of trees fell in Kensington Gardens and the gates were locked for many weeks.

This is part of the jungle at Cheyne Walk. The Royal Borough of Kensington and Chelsea lost more than 800 trees.

A child from Great Ormond Street Hospital amid the devastation in Queen's Square.

Daniel Defore, author of the Great Storm of 1703, is buried in Bunn Hill Cemetery, Finsbury. In 1987 he was disturbed again!

Photograph by David Tippett-Wilson.

A fallen tree causes a traffic jam. This is Somerset Avenue, Hook in the borough of Kingston-upon-Thames.

Fallen trees on the embankment. Tower Bridge is in the background.

Photograph by: N. W. Jackson

Hampstead Heath where devastation gave way to new wide views.

The remains of a mighty oak in Richmond Park.

Photograph by: Mark Davison

The old sycamore has been replaced by a young sapling. This 'before' and 'after' was taken in Watts Road, Thames Ditton.

New views of the city seen through storm damaged branches from Parliament Hill.

The Advertising Standards Authority probably made an exception in this case. Photographer Tim Merry from the Ealing Gazette stumbled on this scene in Churchfield Road. Acton.

Fifteen trees were uprooted in Elm Avenue, Ealing. It could have been renamed Steeplechase Road.

Brent Lodge Park, Ealing has locked its gates to small boys who like climbing fallen trees.

The former press relations officer at Brent Council, Charles Poulter had plenty to tell reporters when a tree fell on his home in Vivian Avenue, Wembley.

An Alperton housewife negotiates an obstacle in Stanley Avenue with the determination of a Londoner.

M4 alert at 2.40am

IT was as early as 2.40am, that John Clack from Hounslow's engineer's department called out a team to clear the M4, and by 4am, teams were being organised to deal with the turmoil in the streets. By 8am, the council had 148 staff and 27 vehicles clearing the main roads. Even the army from Hounslow assisted. Dustcart crews worked until late in the evenings in the days which followed, clearing up after the chainsaw gangs.

THE storm came as a blow to the children at Hogarth Junior School in Chiswick. For the school's logo was the giant old willow which stood in the grounds. Now all that remains is the symbol of the tree on the pupils' tee-shirts. The loss of the willow was just another statistic alongside the 12,000 trees which fell on roads, pavements and parks across the borough of Hounslow, leaving the council with a bill for £1,141,000 before replanting took place.

AFTER days of heavy rain, residents faced a new threat when the River Crane threatened to burst its banks and flood hundreds of homes. A red alert was issued and police prepared to evacuate scores of homes across Hounslow. Damp got into the signals at Boston Manor Park causing major train delays, and a massive lake, 150 feet across, formed on the tracks at Acton North Station. A fleet of taxis was hired by the Underground staff to ferry commuters to their destinations. Although the torrential rain eased in the nick of time, it was too late to stop the Crane overflowing and sweeping through a rubbish tip at Cranford. Tin cans, tea bags and other household garbage, were washed down the streets.

IN February 1988, commemorative planting ceremonies took place at Bedfont Green, Beaversfield Park, Hounslow Heath and Hanworth Park, conducted by Hounslow Council's Leisure Services department as part of a scheme to plant 2000 new trees across the borough.

Three-in-a-row shock for residents of Barrowgate Road, Chiswick. Altogether 15 trees fell in this street.

Fallen birches provide good camouflage for the soldiers of Blenheim Road, Chiswick.

Chiswick High Road near Turnham Green.

Photograph by: Brentford and Chiswick Times

Somewhere in there is Green Dragon Lane at Brentford.

Photograph by: Ealing Gazette

Many trees came down in Syon Park gardens near Brentford and one fell onto the London Butterfly House, built like a greenhouse and kept at tropical temperatures. More than 300 exotic butterflies escaped through the gaping holes where the glass was broken and were swept helplessly across London. Some turned up a few days later in nearby potting sheds, and in an orchard intoxicated by the juice of rotting apples.

Mrs Joy Williamson looks in disbelief at her crumpled Lada car in Balfour Avenue, Hanwell. Joy and her husband Julian have bought a new Lada but they park it well away from the trees.

An unexpected day off and a new adventure playground. This is Churchfields at Hanwell.

Photograph by: John Blandford

Osterley House,

LOOKING over the sun-drenched meadows towards Osterley Park on June 17, 1989, it was hard to imagine that such a ferocious storm could have occurred. Tractors moved at summer's pace, gathering the hay, while the hazy outline of aircraft could be seen ascending from the horizon at Heathrow.

The June 1989 heatwave in Middlesex merely softened the scars of the storm. Beyond the cartwheels of corn, broken boughs of trees criss-crossed the copses. Exactly 20 months earlier the Park was battered by a wind so wretched that 150 trees were gouged out of the ground. Oaks, yews, and planes that had provided shade for many decades, were chiselled from the avenues and glades in one of London's oldest surviving estate parks.

It took National Trust gardeners many months to clear the fallen timber and heavy lifting gear was brought in to lift the logs. This added to the problems, for large ruts were unavoidably left in lawns as the machinery moved to and fro.

Osterley House, the Elizabethan mansion built by Sir Thomas Gresham in 1576, but re-modelled between 1750 and 1780, stood solidly in the teeth of the gale and survived with remarkably little trace of damage.

In the wake of the hurricane, the National Trust held a display of photographs in the house, showing the devastation to the trees in the grounds. A steady stream of tourists to the Adam-designed building gladly dipped into their pockets to help the Trust's Storm Appeal

Osterley Park gardener, Kevin Mills took these pictures of the silver limes in front of the stables before and after the storm.

This Cortina Estate fell foul of a chestnut tree on Twickenham Green near the Salvation Army Citadel.

THE parklands around Hampton were badly disfigured. One thousand trees fell in Home Park and Bushy Park and two years later, local residents were incensed when more chestnut trees were removed near the Diana Fountain in Bushy Park. The authorities tried to reassure them that they had been weakened in the storm and were a danger to the many visitors. The argument raged for many months.

IN Park Road, Teddington, an elderly woman narrowly missed injury when a chimney crashed through her roof and into her bed-sitting room. Being deaf, she did not hear it thunder into her room.

RESIDENTS of a house in Vicarage Road, Hampton Wick, had to be evacuated from their home and given emergency accommodation when two 28-foot chimney stacks became unsafe and threatened to collapse.

KEW Gardens, which lost 1,000 trees and suffered £130,000 worth of damage to buildings alone, was visited by Baroness Trum-pington, the Parliamentary Secretary for the Ministry of Agriculture and Fisheries the following week to see for herself the destruction and to pass on her condolences to those who had years of hard work ruined. A team of horticulturists from Oregon later flew in with chainsaws to help with the clear up operation.

AN unexploded bomb was found in Manor Road, Twickenham — revealed when a tree was upturned. The shell was taken to Twickenham police station where it was later disposed of.

THE Richmond and Twickenham Times reported that among the many hundreds of trees blown down was a 200-year-old copper beech under which William Makepeace Thackeray, as legend has it, wrote parts of Vanity Fair.

"The great writer, whose weighty tomes all tended toward sentimentality, sat beneath the tree scribbling parts of his first and best-known work. It was written seven years after his wife went mad in 1840", said the newspaper.

The famous tree fell across a garden in Rosemont Road, Richmond with the 100-year-old climbing irons still hammered in.

Richmond Park

Photograph by: Richmond and Twickenham Times

Many Richmond people wept with the weeping willows when they saw what the storm had done. Artist Jennifer Wyatt captured the tragedy on canvas.

RICHMOND Park on a warm summer's afternoon is the playground of Londoners. Weary of the hot dusty streets and tiresome traffic, they flock to the park's wide open spaces, grassy hillocks and rhododendron gardens.

The hurricane also visited the park's 2,358 acres. Screaming at close-on 100 mph, the winds gouged out hundreds of oak trees dating back more than 200 years. Herds of fallow deer and red deer were doubtless terrified as the mighty oaks fell, shaking the ground where they were huddled together.

The gale ripped through the famous plantations, rendering them so dangerous, the public were kept out for some three to four months afterwards.

At first light, the full scale of havoc could be seen by the park wardens. It seemed in those stunning first impressions that irreparable damage had been caused. This was a view shared by Roy Smith, chairman of the Friends of Richmond Park.

Immediately, the Friends launched a tree appeal, and the response from the 2000 members was magnificent, with £3,000 being raised to help replace some of the 1,145 trees uprooted.

On February 17, 1988, stalwart members turned up in the dawn rain and drizzle to plant the first tree. It was planted just inside Roehampton Gate, and marked the first of many such occasions.

The great storm helped to strengthen the aims of the Friends who encourage the preservation of Richmond Park.

Photographs by: Department of Medical Illustration

Before . . . . and after the hurricane. Prior to October 1987, the leafy square beneath St. Bartholomew's Hospital in West Smithfield, provided some visual relief from London's concrete jungles as seen in this 1951 picture. In one night all the trees were so badly damaged they had to be cut down. Two of London's oldest planes didn't need a helping hand; they were lying on their sides at first light. A 'Square Appeal' fund was later established.

A drama without the crisis

WHEN a tower block on the North Peckham Estate seemed in danger of collapsing, Dulwich Hospital was put on emergency standby in case of a disaster. Families were evacuated and experts called in to examine the concrete pillars supporting the skyscraper. Miraculously all was well.

Despite such a night of wholesale destruction, there were remarkably few casualties. If there had been more, then the crisis in the wards would have been acute for many nurses and doctors found their route to work blocked by trees and debris.

As power cuts plunged London into darkness hospitals lost their supplies for a few seconds until emergency generators started up. One or two failed and nurses toured the wards with candles and food cooked on gas stoves.

For some hospitals it was a night the nurses and doctors will never forget, with chimneys crashing into wards, and shattered windows bursting over patients.

☐ Queen Charlotte's and Chelsea Hospital was totally blacked out when an emergency generator failed due to a starting motor defect. By a strange stroke of luck, mothers expecting to give birth that night did so before the power cut, and there were no births during the 4½ hours the supply was off.

In the hospital's neonatal unit, where babies on ventilators rely on electricity to operate the machines, staff used the manual ventilation procedure, which though tedious, was carried out successfully with no ill effects to the infants.

☐ Windows were blown out at St. Stephens Hospital, Chelsea, leaving the Pharmacy department 'vulnerable'.

☐ A brick-built gable end wall at West Middlesex University Hospital in Isleworth was blown out. A plant room door in the roof area had been left open and the build-up of internal pressure forced the wall to collapse outwards. The hospital's storm bill came to £10,000.

☐ Forty calls were made to the emergency works department at Northwick Park Hospital, Harrow, as windows shattered and trees fell causing structural damage. A duct from the mortuary was blown off its mountings.

☐ A tree smashed through the roof of the newly-built Firs ward at High Wood Hospital, Brentwood, and 50 trees were uprooted.

☐ Three greenhouses, two sheds, and 61 trees out of 101 at Manor Hospital, Epsom, were destroyed.

☐ Patients were evacuated from high level wards at Ealing Hospital in Southall after steel corrugated cladding was progressively torn off a service tower block on the 11th, 12th and 13th floors. The flying debris posed such a danger that the windows in the patient areas had to be internally boarded up with plywood half an inch thick. All the cladding fixings had to be removed and replaced at a considerable cost.

☐ At 4.20am, South Western Hospital in Stockwell was in darkness as London's power failed. The emergency generators came on, and in the dim lights, the elderly and confused patients were reassured. After seven hours without proper power, fears grew that fuel for the generators would not last. They had only 1½ hours' supply left when the lights came on again at 11.25am.

Meanwhile, the hurricane lifted a 25 square metre pitched roof off the water tower and hurled it through the corridor ceiling below, blocking the route to the kitchens. The wind had got into the tower after windows were sucked out by its force. Coping stones and heavy slabs also rained down into the kitchen passage. Elsewhere, 12 windows were smashed and extensive damage was caused to guttering, fences and roof tiles. Nearly 80 of the 100 trees in the gardens were ripped apart, or uprooted.

It was a night that the unit works officer, Robert Midgley has firmly etched in his mind. He drove out into the night from his home in Enfield and headed for the hospital. After numerous diversions around Bush Hill Park and later the Homerton one way system, he eventually arrived at Liverpool Street, where shuttering and debris were flying around as his car was blown from side to side of the road. He looked up and saw a woman police constable clinging to traffic lights for all she was worth. Then she was bowled across the road. He asked if she was all right, She said she was, and waved him on.

☐ Goodmayes Hospital lost 166 trees. Its sports and social club was struck by a falling tree which smashed a window. It took 308 working days to clear the trees, which included 52 ash, 20 hawthorn and 14 black Italian poplars. From the hospital, staff can now see Kent across the river.

☐ The theatre roof at Sydenham Children's Hospital was hit by a tree causing damage and glass was shattered in another part of the hospital roof.

☐ The North Middlesex Hospital in Edmonton's Stirling Way was one of the worst affected in London. The main gate was blocked and the pharmacy department roof was wrecked, but queues of off-duty Nurses offered their services next morning despite a complete cessation of public transport in North London. Some casualties arrived with storm-related cuts and bruises.

☐ Elderly patients at Green Trees Hospital in Tottenhall Road, Palmers Green were lying in bed when chimney pots crashed through the ceiling into the wards just feet from where they were asleep.

☐ An open window was wrenched off its hinges at Purley Hospital, Staff had to make extensive detours to get to work.

☐ A male patient at St. Christopher's Hospice in Lawrie Park Road, Sydenham, was unharmed when a window was blown in on to his bed. The emergency generators failed, but staff coped 'excellently with candles, improvisation and gas cooking'.

☐ Cane Hill Hospital for the mentally ill at Coulsdon was bombarded by flying debris and falling trees, resulting in a clear-up bill for £100,000. Built in 1883 as one of the outer London mental asylums, it is now scheduled for closure by the Bromley Area Health Authority.

☐ A trainee girl engineer at Atkinson Morley's Hospital in Wimbledon was injured, and her boyfriend's leg was broken when a chimney and bricks cascaded down on their bed in an attic room of an old house in The Drive, Wimbledon. They were treated in St. George's, Tooting.

☐ Damage to the hospital buildings at the Joyce Green Hospital, Dartford, came to £130,000. Four nurses' homes had to be partially re-roofed and numerous windows were blown out. Glass covered walkways were wrecked and 100 trees blown down, blocking entrances. Forty terrified elderly patients were evacuated from Trafalgar ward when the roof was ripped off. They had to be taken in wheelchairs through the howling gale to the main hospital building.

God made the decisions at Hampton Court

THE ghostly wails that shrieked through Hampton Court Palace in the small hours of October 16, 1987, were not the spirits of Henry VIII's wives but screaming gusts of the wildest winds ever known.

The palace is said to be haunted by the ghosts of Anne Boleyn and Jane Seymour, but on that dreadful night in 1987 any apparitions were overshadowed by the storm around the Palace and nearby Home Park.

More than 800 trees, some dating back to the time of Charles II and William III, creaked, groaned, and then fell like dominoes in the historic grounds. The famous avenues of centuries-old limes were torn down and boundary walls, built during the reigns of Henry VIII and William III were, in places, reduced to rubble.

Assistant gardens and estates manager, Mr Terry Gough lay in bed at his home in Home Park listening to the howling storm. Suddenly, the landing light, left on for his two young sons, blacked out. Fearing for the safety of the Palace, he picked up the telephone to speak to other staff, but could not get through. He distinctly remembers hearing a cross-line conversation in which the words hurricane and devastation were used.

At first light he left his house and walked towards the Palace. The air was filled with the smell of tree sap; so strong was the odour that Mr Gough will remember it clearly for years.

Nearly every road was impassable; there was carnage everywhere. In the year that followed, a massive clear-up operation started on what Mr Gough described as Mother Nature's enforced forestry work. "God had made all the decisions that people had been thinking about for 25 years," he said. "It enabled a major restoration programme to be drawn up. It forced our hand. Although it was a disaster we acted positively".

An agreement was drawn up with pulp timber firms and much of the wood was removed by September 1988 to Wales. The poor quality timber was used for paper manufacture and the better trees were sent off for mining timber. A good sum was raised from the sale.

The replanting will be helped by a donation from the Prince Charles storm appeal and some of the lime avenues may be replaced in time.

As for the structural damage, minor repair work to the Palace was soon put in hand with repair teams replacing fallen guttering and tiles on outbuildings.

The Palace's own team of six specialist brick workers repaired walls, sometimes using hand-made bricks to restore the boundaries authentically.

Boathouse destroyed

ONE of the River Thames' historic boathouses built by the legendary Tom Tagg in the 1800s was destroyed in the gale. The building was scooped up by the wind and hurled on to the Barge Walk outside Hampton Court Palace. Remarkably, the 30 boats inside were almost unscathed, but thousands of pounds worth of damage was caused to the structure of the building.

Photograph by: G. Cooke

This photograph says something above the strength of the wind in Hampton Court Gardens. A major restoration programme was immediately drawn up.

Police stations throughout London were besieged with telephone calls from householders, pedestrians and motorists but there was little that could be done until a list of priority hazards had been established. Here, an officer comes face to face with a villain in Balham Park Road.

A chopped up, towering oak outside Hanworth Library. One day it might be inside!

Photographs by: Hounslow, Feltham and Hanworth Times

Chaos in Feltham High Street on the morning of the storm was caused by this oak tree which brought traffic to a halt.

Roehampton's famous storm. October 15, 1780

LEWIS Brown, a gardener lived in a house alongside the lane to Barnes Common. A violent wind arose and suddenly the upper part of the house was forced out and formed a chasm in the room where his daughter lay. Luckily the bricks fell outwards and she escaped injury.

The barn and other out-buildings were levelled to the ground and one person was killed while another died later. Debris was scattered far and wide. A body of a large cart was torn from its wheels and flung a distance of 90 paces. A large walnut tree 12 feet in circumference was torn up by the roots and whisked 22 feet from the hole where it had grown.

Roehampton Lane was a scene of utter devastation with 130 trees, some very large, torn down and the avenue they had formed totally destroyed. They lay to the north and north-west across the road which was impassable for a month. One 40 foot tree is said to have been lifted and carried 130 yards to the north side of the road upon Barnes Common. Sightseers later remarked that the earth in adjoining fields had been torn up and gave the appearance of having been ploughed.

The work-house upon Barnes Common lost its chimneys and the windmill was hurled upside down and smashed to pieces. The storm covered an area three miles long beginning at Lord Belborough's at Roehampton and ending in Hammersmith, where the church was badly hit. At no point was it more than 200 yards wide. Vast crowds came for several days to see the turmoil.

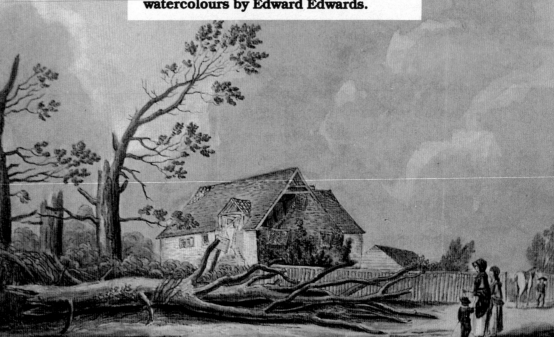

A storm of exceptional ferocity which hit Roehampton and Barnes on October 15, 1780 is captured in these watercolours by Edward Edwards.

Drought — a new peril

THE Great Storm was a sudden and vicious affair, exacting an immense toll in fallen trees, changing habitats for wildlife and, in small and large gardens, destroying in minutes plants carefully nurtured through the years.

Just when replanting and restoration was beginning to show results a more insidious yet potentially just as damaging element of Nature was to reveal itself in 1989.

The winter of 1988/89 was both warm and dry, with the temperature reaching 16c(61f) in early February. Normally this is the time of the year when moisture is returned to the soil left thirsty after summer evaporation. This year it remained dry and dusty. Worse was to follow as a sunny May proved to be the driest this century with less than two mm of rain in some parts of London.

Mr David Frost of the London Tree Officers Association and the Arboricultural Officer for Ealing stated that the 32 London Boroughs had planted more than 100,000 trees to replace those lost in the storm. They were lacking a well established root-system and had to bear the brunt of the dry conditions which continued right through the summer.

Richmond Council in S.W. London appealed to ratepayers to each give a bucketful of water to it's 2000 new trees. Ealing mounted an emergency watering operation with a fleet of 500 gallon tankers and extra staff. The council had been wise and laid a pipe direct to the root base of every tree.

The Tree Council insisted that thorough watering was needed; a mere sprinkle on the surface forced roots to travel upwards only to perish in the dry conditions.

Photograph by: R. Tilley

Throughout the long hot summer of 1989, London Fire Brigade experienced their busiest period of grass fires since 1976. Flames roared across London's parks and commons and at one stage, the Brigade was answering up to 800 calls a day, six times their normal amount. In the drought trees were damaged or destroyed in the fires. Here, firemen tackle a bush fire which swept Nonsuch Park in the London Borough of Sutton on June 21st 1989.

Four years of crazy weather

- January '85 was bitterly cold and snow lay on the ground in Kensington for two weeks. At Morden the temperature was minus 10C.

- Dismal summer of '85 was enlivened at Wimbledon when lightning struck the centre court. Torrential rain with hail unloaded 50mm (2 inches) in less than an hour.

- November '85 coldest in some parts of London since 1923. At Coulsdon the mercury stayed below freezing all day on the 19th.

- Christmas '85 was not white but wet, very wet. West Norwood was drenched with 47mm (1¾ inches), making it their wettest festive season ever.

- February '86 the second coldest this century (after 1947). London littered with broken down lorries as diesel fuel froze.

- August '86 ex-hurricane Charlie left his calling card at Kensington when 25mm (1 inch) fell on Bank Holiday Monday.

- September '86 a bizarre month. Plenty of sunshine, half the average rainfall and exceedingly cold. Four ground frosts at Morden. October was warmer than September — a rare event.

- New Year '87 warm and promising. Temperature of 52F at Stockwell and West Norwood. Talk of an intense mass of cold air heading from Eastern Europe.

- January '87 and bitterly cold. Heavy snow showers. West Norwood's coldest day of the century. Conditions close to Siberia as 375mm (15 inches) falls on hillier parts of London. Big Ben freezes and chimes stop. Thames ices over from Runnymede to Sunbury. Clouds of crystalline snow sweep across every borough. Police advise everyone to stay at home. Terrible thaws follow. Plumbers answer 1,000 calls a day for help.

- March '87 and dust from Sahara falls with rain at Morden. Severe gales. Three men crushed to death at Banstead as tree falls on van. Old Bailey dome damaged by wind. Severe thunderstorms with hail.

- October '87 begins as wettest of the century. At Cricklewood 200mm (8 inches) of rain falls. Flood water reaches three feet in depth on North Circular at Golders Green. London Fire Brigade takes 527 calls in four hours. Wimbledon to West Croydon railway line under water. In Waltham Forest the borough emergency plan swings into operation.

- October '87 and the Great Storm. Hurricane force winds but not officially a hurricane.

- January '88 and the wettest of the century in South London. Borough of Croydon buys expensive snow-blower but it fails to snow.

- Christmas '88 and London is as warm as Malaga, Rome and Athens. Croydon's snow-blower gathers more cobwebs.

- February '89. The lowest air pressure since 1821 measured.

- April 5th 1989 recorded the coldest day of the winter with up to 100mm (4 inches) of snow on the higher parts of South London.

- May '89. Driest May ever recorded.

- Summer of '89. Severe droughts and restrictions placed on use of hoses. Water rationing introduced and many forest fires. London's sunniest summer of the century.

In the London borough of Sutton, Bankside Close lies in a wooded hollow at Carshalton. Residents were trapped for days and the only way out for cars was via the sky.

443 lost — 500 planted

MAYOR of Kingston in the storm year was Mrs Jenny Philpott who appealed to everyone to help the borough regain its much-loved and characteristic leafy land-scape. By spring the following year thousands of pounds had been collected and more than 500 trees planted to replace the 443 lost overnight.

KINGSTON'S civic dignitaries attended many tree-planting ceremonies including one at the King Edward recreation ground at Hook where, in the 1920's, Enid Blyton, the author, used to take her pupils for nature studies while running a kindergarten in Hook Road.

AT Chessington Zoo two huge marquees were shredded and at Tolworth Infants and Junior School the main tiled roof was so badly damaged that £86,000 had to be spent on repairs. At Tiffin Girls School in Richmond Road a sheet of aluminium roof was torn off.

THE Guildhall, where the council set up an emergency control room, had to be roped off. £77,000 of damage occurred.

Photograph by: David Tippett-Wilson

Hook is one of the southernmost districts in Greater London. Lying at just 100 feet above the level of the Thames, the parish escaped some of the brutal gusts which devastated other more hilly areas. However, many roads were littered with debris, and in Somerset Avenue, Woodstock Lane and Elm Road, fallen trees blocked roads. This picture was taken in Elm Road.

Michael Fish was not to blame

BBC weatherman Michael Fish, who had assured TV viewers the previous day that there would not be a hurricane, is pictured here with Mrs Elizabeth Southey at his first public engagement after the event. He was talking to the Surrey Federation of Women's Institutes at Dorking. Mr Fish said the woman who telephoned the BBC to ask if there was a hurricane on the way, was referring to "a completely different depression". It wasn't just Mr Fish's pride that was damaged, for fences around his Middlesex home were flattened. His drive to work at the London Weather Centre was easier than normal that morning 'because there were no cars on the road', he said. The woman who rang the BBC to ask about the possibility of a hurricane was Mrs Anita Hart of Pinner, Middlesex. An official inquiry into the catastrophe cleared Michael Fish of any blame, but criticised the Met. Office Staff for sticking too rigidly to computer guidance.

A bees nest in a tree at Ashford Manor Golf Course near Heathrow Airport was thrown into turmoil when the tree thudded to the ground. Golfers managed to save the nest by building a hive over the horizontal trunk. Pictured with the hive is Barbara Edwards, the former BBC weather forecaster who is a keen golfer at Ashford.

Photograph by Dorking Advertiser

In many places the terrain was too rough for tractors and a more traditional method of removing timber was employed. Here at Sydenham Hill Wood, Dulwich are two heavy Ardennes horses.

The hurricane led to many outdoor nature lessons for school children, and here, the deputy head teacher of Hasmonean Prep School in Shirehall Lane, Hendon, explains the root system of a fallen tree.

Horror in Holland Park

MORE than 300 trees, many of them rare species, fell in Holland Park, Kensington. Only ten out of 80 were left in Lime Avenue and not a single tree in Chestnut Avenue escaped damage. Saddest of all was the loss of the favourites. A mulberry by the sandpit, two Pride of Indias by the Ice House and the fountain and the Tree of Heaven opposite the Belvedere Restaurant. Only one branch was left on the Indian Bean Tree (catalpa bignonioides) and the Friends of Holland Park did what they could to save this "gallant old survivor". By March 1988 the clearing up had been completed and 200 new trees planted at a cost of £16,000.

Children from South London in Kensington's Holland Park. With them is Cr Mrs Elizabeth Russell, mayor of Kensington and Chelsea Royal Borough at the time of the storm.

Lime Avenue, Holland Park — 90 per cent damage.

Photograph by: Surrey Comet

Photograph by Fern Flunn

The famous Pagoda which towers 163 feet above Kew Gardens came through unscathed but the historic gardens were badly damaged. More than 500 trees fell and a further 500 torn to shreds. The Tree of Heaven fell on William IV's temple but other picturesque buildings survived. The gardens had to be closed for 12 days and parts remained closed for several months until dangerous trees had been felled and hanging limbs removed. Kew is recovering fast. Many trees have been re-established by propogation. Careful nurturing of seedlings and saplings will ensure that the gaps are filled.

*The hurricane was, for better or worse, an entirely
natural catastrophe, an integral part of the workings of
the environment, not some alien force. Similar storms
have probably torn across England's woods 20 times
since they first became established, and yet they still
managed to survive.*

Richard Mabey
chairman of the London Wildlife Trust, writing in BBC Wildlife

Photograph by: Dominic Dibbs, British Trust Conservation Volunteers.

*From little acorns mighty oaks will grow. Children from Peterborough Junior School at Bishop's Palace in
Fulham during National Tree Week, 1987.*

About the Authors

*Mark Davison with
BBC weatherman, John Kettley*

Ian Currie with David Bellamy

Mark Davison

MARK Davison is deputy editor of the Surrey Mirror Series and a keen amateur meteorologist who has an amazing photographic collection of extreme weather conditions from snowstorms and fogs to protracted droughts, heatwaves and hailstorms. He is also joint author, with Ian Currie, of the book *Surrey In The Hurricane* which was a county bestseller and has raised almost £8,000 for the Surrey Wildlife Trust.

Ian Currie

IAN Currie has spent all his working life as a teacher of geography and meteorology. He is well known for his weekly weather column in the Surrey Mirror, Sutton Herald and Surrey Comet series of newspapers and is heard each week on Radio Redhill. He is a Fellow of the Royal Meteorological Society and he has an Open University Degree based on geography and earth science. Ian reestablished the meteorology section of the Croydon Natural History and Scientific Society in Croydon, and has acted as a consultant on meteorological matters to various local firms.

3805

Hurricane Books from Froglets

In the Wake of the Hurricane (Kent Edition)	ISBN 0-9513019-0-X	£7.00
In the Wake of the Hurricane (National)	ISBN 0-9513019-1-8	£7.50
In the Wake of the Hurricane (Hardback)	ISBN 0-9513019-4-2	£11.95
Surrey in the Hurricane	ISBN 0-9513019-2-6	£7.50
Hurricane Gilbert	ISBN 0-9513019-5-0	£7.50
An Eye on The Hurricane (Eastern Counties)	ISBN 0-9513019-6-9	£7.95
Eastern Counties (Hardback)	ISBN 0-9513019-7-7	£11.95
King Oak of Sevenoaks	ISBN 1-872337-00-7	£8.95

What the papers say

London's Hurricane joins the family of hurricane books. This is what the critics said of the earlier editions, written by Bob Ogley.

Literary fate has made him a star — something he declines being at his roots a countryman who has pumped his typewriter and cracked his staff into action over the past 18 years. Because of demand In The Wake of The Hurricane is more elusive than Spycatcher.
— **Exeter Express and Echo.**

As a record of the power of nature mocking the efforts of man and as a reminder of the vulnerability of things we take so much for granted this is an awesome volume.
— **Kev Reynolds, Environment Now**

Among writers, the patriarch and forerunner of all chroniclers of the storm is Bob Ogley, editor of the local paper in Sevenoaks, Kent.
— **The Times.**

This first book on the hurricane adds flesh to the bones of the growing legend of the night of October 16, 1987.
— **Express and Star, Wolverhampton.**

An album of reports and photographs of the devastation on a scale more familiar with the Far East and the Caribbean. Bob Ogley's sensational collection is a reminder of the need to restore as well as rebuild.
— **The Guardian.**

Bob Ogley has captured the century's worst storm with this magnificent best selling book.
— **Frank Thompson, Daily Mail**

What an inspired idea to cover the hurricane's trail. This really is a magnificent book.
— **Group Capt Sir Leonard Cheshire VC**

In the Wake Of The Hurricane has a dramatic array of pictures, some of which were taken from a plane which Bob Ogley hired. He was especially well-placed to mourn the falling of Sevenoaks' eponymous trees.
— **The Independent.**

Bob experienced every waking minute in the teeth of the storm and wrote a best seller, In The Wake of The Hurricane. He is an ardent conservationist — a man who has spent nearly all his life immersed in the countryside.
— **Bob Bryant, Gloucester Citizen.**

A first class production and an excellent record of the devastation that hit our part of Kent on the night of October 16, 1987. Bob Ogley has put it together with great speed and commendable skill.
— **Winston S Churchill, Western**

Bob Ogley's bright idea for a book on the hurricane meant a victory over condescending publishers.
— **Michael O'Flaherty, Daily Express.**

The success of his collection of vivid photographs and dramatic text was immediate; the book became number two in the paperback list. Sceptical publishers had given no encouragement.
— **Rachel Warren, Evening Standard.**

The book has sold a staggering 90,000 copies in eight months, broken sales records in Kent, spent many weeks in the bestsellers lists and raised £40,000 for charity.
— **Mike Swain, Today.**

"We chroniclers of the storm all stand in debt to Bob Ogley in much the same degree as all other epic poets stand in debt to Homer"
— **George Hill, Hurricane Force.**

"It is indeed a remarkable record of a dreadful night and a record which will become part of the history of our country"
— **Denis and Margaret Thatcher, 10 Downing Street.**